Walking With, Watc...

Taking time to go for a walk is one of life's g... peace may help us to solve a problem or see things differently – especially if we can walk and talk with a companion or keep silence together.

It is summer in the northern hemisphere during this quarter. The more relaxed schedule in the warm weather means (for those who are able) that there may be time to go for a walk – perhaps on the beach or in the woods.

'Walking with' is a form of Christian discipline. In my own denomination we understand our relationships within the church as 'walking with' one another – in other words, we follow Jesus together through the variety of life's experiences. We're also committed to 'watching over' one another: caring for one another's wellbeing. 'Watching over' may mean challenging as well as being supportive, since we are called by a holy God to a way of life that speaks of him.

Our notes in this issue often bring these two ideas of *walking* and *watching* to mind. For example, *walking with a friend* aptly describes the disciples' experience of being with Jesus. Another example is

walking under God's law, law given to bless us and not to limit us. If we have ever walked in dangerous places, we will have learned that guidelines are usually there to help us.

Perhaps you will identify with walking with your shoes off. It is a different, unmediated encounter with the physical world. Our God is holy, and we should tread respectfully when we encounter him.

How is your walk today? Perhaps you are moving through spacious places; or perhaps life has delivered a curve ball and you are limping in pain. Either way, our dearest companion walks with and watches over us, never abandoning us. Even if he moves on ahead, it is to show us the way. His Word is a trustworthy light unto our feet.

Sally Nelson
Editor

Isaac O'Brien
Content Assistant

ON THE COVER: '... hold fast to that lamp and keep it close beside me so that ... God might guide and lead me safely along his path of life' (pages 72 to 75)

Image credit: Shutterstock / Svetliy

The Writers

TANYA FERDINANDUSZ is both a freelance writer and freelance editor, and has been writing Bible reading notes, articles and devotionals for over 25 years. She is a Bible study leader and the author of *Marriage Matters*, a book for Christian couples.

STUART WEIR is passionate about Jesus Christ and sport. He spends his life helping people to make the connection. In his seventies he still plays walking football regularly. He has worked at four football World Cups and Paris 2024 will be his fifth accredited Olympic involvement. Married to Lynne for 50 years, he has two children and three grandchildren.

FIONA BARNARD loves being with people from all over the world as an ESOL (English for Speakers of Other Languages) tutor, the University of St Andrews' chaplain and Friends International staff worker. She lives in Scotland.

ANDREW HERON worked as a government translator before training for Christian ministry. He subsequently worked in missionary service in France for almost 25 years, then latterly in pastoral ministry in Northern Ireland.

KATHARINE MCPHAIL and husband Stuart have two grown-up children. Katharine and Stuart feel called to serve in church ministry together. They were both at Hill Cliffe Baptist Church for 10 years until Katharine felt called to train for Baptist ministry. She is currently at Hoole Baptist Church in Chester on placement.

SALLY NELSON is the Dean of Baptist Formation at St Hild College, Yorkshire, where she also teaches Christian doctrine and pastoral care. She is a Baptist minister and has been the commissioning editor for *Encounter with God* since 2015.

ISAAC O'BRIEN is a Content Assistant at Scripture Union and the content manager of *Encounter with God*. He is passionate about the Bible, theology and Jesus, and loves leading worship in church.

Contents

Scripture Union is a member of the worldwide Scripture Union international community.
Website: https://scriptureunion.global

SPORT SPEAKS OF GOD

Sport has huge appeal among young people and provides unique opportunities to connect with them, build relationships and share Jesus. Thanks to your support, we are able to help more churches than ever before to use this amazing medium for mission!

Scripture Union Sports Mission Team Leader Mark Oliver and his team – Sarah Bowey, Ruth Anderson and Holly Phipps – want every church in England and Wales to be able to make the most of the mission opportunities that sport can offer, whether that's just throwing a frisbee round the local park or running a sports-themed camp.

Mark says, 'We all have a responsibility to tell the next generation about Jesus. As we engage with children and young people, it's important that we do so in a way that is accessible to them. With more children and young people playing sport every Sunday than attending church, we know that sport speaks a language that they understand.'

A broad appeal to young people

Not every young person would consider themselves to be 'sporty' and Mark is keen to point out that in the context of mission, '... we're not just talking about competitive, conventional or organised sports such as football, netball or tennis. We include simple and fun physical games and activities too, things that appeal to most young people and require no previous experience to play.

'Mission Through Sport brings the community together and helps young people from a variety of backgrounds to develop skills and confidence that are useful both on and off the pitch. It builds relationships and so provides a way in to sharing the good news about Jesus.'

Flexibility suits a range of church settings

Mission Through Sport can also be readily adapted to most contexts.

Mark says, 'We've trained our Mission Enablers so that they can help Faith Guides run sports mission easily and effectively, whether they're from a big church with access to a playing field or a small rural church with more limited local facilities, or anything in between.'

The team is also developing new off-the-shelf resources for churches to use. These are based on the Revealing Jesus mission framework. 'So, whether a church is connecting with young people for the first time, or helping them to explore faith, respond or grow spiritually, these Mission Through Sport resources will help,' explains Mark. 'For example, we've created a series of "Half Time" talks with videos and accompanying games which Faith Guides can use to share something from the Bible, linked to a games session. We're also developing an additional set of videos that the young people can access in their own time, which help them explore that week's theme in more depth.

'For those Faith Guides who want to go a step further and specialise in Mission Through Sport, we're developing an accredited training course so they can construct their own programmes that are specifically tailored to the needs of the young people they work with.

'Mission Through Sport is amazingly flexible – we really love showing churches how to make it a success in their particular circumstances!'

A missional game-changer

Having piloted lots of 'estate-based' sports programmes in the past few years, SU's Sports Mission Team is leading the way in supporting churches in low-income neighbourhoods to step out and reach the local children and young people.

Mark's passion is rooted in Isaiah 61 where we are instructed to 'proclaim good news to the poor'. He says, 'In such communities where I've worked, alongside the economic challenges, I've witnessed a poverty of hope. What greater hope is there than knowing Jesus? But a much higher proportion of churches in low-income communities have closed their doors than in affluent areas. We can use sports, games and fitness activities to make connections with children and young people and introduce them to Jesus. It can literally be a missional game-changer!

'It is such a privilege to work alongside churches and congregation members living and working on those estates. They are so willing to roll up their sleeves and get out into their communities and share God's love in practical ways.'

More intensive help

Getting Mission Through Sport programmes off the ground in these areas is not always plain sailing and the churches involved often appreciate the extra practical help they can get from Mark and his team.

Holly Phipps is one of SU's two Sports Mission Pioneers and is based in Sheffield. She's been working with All Nations, a church founded on the Fir Vale estate in September 2022. In Easter 2023, Holly and Mark partnered with a team of church volunteers and Christians in Sport to run a three-day sports camp to connect with local young people. Over 30 came. They included Josh*, who arrived on the first day to see his friends who were at the event. Sadly, his attitude was disrespectful and his actions disruptive.

Mark says, 'My instinct was to send Josh home, but I felt that God had other plans. I decided to invite him back the next day on the condition that he got his parents to complete a consent form and that he

* Name changed to protect identity

changed his attitude. To my surprise, he returned.'

'I think I need Jesus to change me'

However, Josh's conduct was even more challenging on day two. 'He was resistant to everything we were doing to the point that his behaviour was spoiling things for everyone else,' recalls Mark. 'I spent time talking with him and could see that he had potential, but I didn't know how to get through to him.'

Nevertheless, Josh returned on the final day of the sports camp as Mark was preparing to share the good news of Jesus. 'It was one of the toughest groups I've ever had to face, but as I began speaking, the group went really quiet.

'At the end, I asked them to get into pairs and a member of the team went to speak with each pair. I found myself talking to Josh. He'd been really affected by the message I'd shared and what he said next was amazing: "I think I need Jesus to change me." And he meant it.

'Hearing that after the challenges of the previous days made it all worthwhile. Josh didn't become a Christian that day, but he did encounter hope and love on

a sports field and now attends weekly sports sessions delivered by our team and the local church. God's love had started to dismantle the seemingly impenetrable wall of resistance that Josh had built around himself.

'Sport really can reach the hearts that other kinds of mission might not reach. My prayer is that many more churches will come to realise its value in sharing Jesus with a generation that doesn't yet know him.'

Please pray for Mark and the Scripture Union Sport team as they seek to help children and young people to learn more about Jesus. If you are interested in learning more about Mission Through Sport, visit su.org.uk/sport

A shorter version of this story first appeared in *Connecting You*, SU's free quarterly supporter magazine. If you'd like to receive copies of *Connecting You* and learn more of how God is moving in the hearts and lives of children and young people today, you can sign up online at su.org.uk/connectingyou.

Using this Guide

Encounter with God is designed for thinking Christians who want to interpret and apply the Bible in a way that is relevant to the problems and issues of today's world. It is based on the NIV translation of the Bible, but can easily be used with any other version.

Each set of readings begins with an *Introduction* to the section you are about to study. The *Call to Worship* section at the start of each note should help you consciously to come into God's presence before you read the passage. The main *Explore* section aims to bring out the riches hidden in the text. The *Growing in Faith* section at the end suggests ways of applying the message to daily living.

The *Bible in a Year* readings at the foot of the page are for those who want this additional option.

INFORMED CHOICE

Health-care professionals provide patients with information about diagnosis, prognosis and treatment options, so that patients can make informed choices. John gives his readers the information they need to make an informed choice about Jesus: 'these are written that you may believe that Jesus is the Messiah'.[1]

These early chapters of John diagnose the human condition and offer a prognosis and treatment plan! The diagnosis is grim: we stand 'condemned' because we have chosen 'darkness' and 'evil' (3:18–20). The prognosis, however, is promising because of Jesus, the giver of both 'light' and 'eternal life' (1:4,5,9; 3:15,16). He alone is the remedy for our sin-sickness. John's Gospel announces the *availability* of this treatment and emphasises the necessity of *availing* ourselves of it. As repeated emphasis on the verb 'believe' suggests (eg 1:12; 2:11; 3:16,36), informed consent is expressed by affirming our trust in Jesus.

John's prologue spells out the fundamental choice that sets sin-sick people on the road to recovering life: 'to all who did receive him, to those who believed in his name,he gave the right to become children of God' (1:12). Varying images present this basic choice: come-and-see invitations, which must be accepted or rejected (1:35–51); welcoming the one to whom the signs point, as opposed to remaining stuck at the signpost (2:11,23,24); being born from above or clinging to familiar things below (3:5–12); being satisfied with temporary thirst-quenchers versus drinking the 'living water' (4:10–15); settling for physical healing as opposed to pursuing wholeness (5:14); craving bread that fills the stomach or feeding on the living bread that satisfies the soul (6:26–58). All these choices have eternal implications: 'while we are free to choose our actions, we are not free to choose the consequences of those actions'.[2] Jesus and John urge us to make not just life-giving but *eternal-life*-giving choices.

Tanya Ferdinandusz

---

[1] John 20:31 [2] Stephen Covey, *The 7 Habits of Highly Effective People*, Simon & Schuster, 2004, p90

John 6:1–15

Factor in Jesus

What presses heavily on your heart today? Will you 'Let petitions and praises shape your worries into prayers, letting God know your concerns'?[1]

The 'great crowd' approaching Jesus would need food – *lots* of it (v 5). Demand far exceeded supply. The immensity of this pressing need, combined with the inadequacy of available resources, overwhelmed the disciples.

Philip was problem-focused. He concentrated on *how* to feed this multitude and his calculations were probably spot on: 'more than half a year's wages to buy enough bread for each one to have a bite!' (v 7). Andrew seems more solution-focused. Yet, having assessed the available resources – 'five small barley loaves and two small fish' – he despaired: 'how far will they go among so many?' (v 9). Philip was daunted by the huge demand; Andrew was sceptical about the meagre supply.

Jesus devised a little 'test' (v 6), presumably to see if his disciples had learned to focus on the *who* rather than the *where* or *how*. Yet, despite having watched their Master perform many wonders, both Philip and Andrew failed to factor Jesus into the equation. In contrast to the disciples, who focused on what seemed an insurmountable problem, Jesus looked up to his Father with thanksgiving and trust (v 11). Giving thanks is far more than an expression of gratitude for gifts; it is also recognition of the greatness of the *Giver* of all good gifts. Giving thanks was followed by giving out (distributing) the bread and trusting God to meet the great need. Philip only thought in terms of 'a bite' (v 7) – a little snack to stave off those hunger pangs! – but Jesus provided not just 'enough' but abundantly (vs 12,13)! As Paul reminds the Philippians, God meets all our needs not *out of* but 'according to' – that is, in proportion to – his great 'riches'.[2]

Problems may seem insurmountable. Our strength may fail. But God reminds us, 'My grace is enough; it's all you need. My strength comes into its own in your weakness.'[3]

[1] Phil 4:6, *The Message* [2] Phil 4:19 [3] 2 Cor 12:9, *The Message*

BIBLE IN A YEAR: **2 Chronicles 33,34; Psalms 75,76**

Under His Feet

'We have an anchor that keeps the soul / steadfast and sure while the billows roll; / fastened to the Rock which cannot move, / grounded firm and deep in the Saviour's love!'[1]

Rowing across the Sea of Galilee, with darkness falling, winds howling and waves rising high (vs 17,18), must have been terrifying for the disciples. In the midst of the storm, what a spectacularly frightening sight it must have been to see Jesus walking towards them on the water!

Most people, knowing the unpredictability of the sea, have a healthy fear of it. For the ancient Jews, it was more than this, because the sea symbolised the forces of chaos which could not be controlled or contained by human beings. Anyone able to command the sea was seen as exercising divine power. Some Old Testament figures received God's power to part the waters,[2] but no one had ever walked on water as Jesus did: '[God] alone … treads on the waves of the sea'.[3] By declaring, 'It is I' (v 20), Jesus associated himself with that divine 'I AM' who appeared to Moses in the burning bush[4] – an identification made more explicit in his 'I am the bread of life' discourse that takes up the rest of chapter 6. In the presence of the divine, human beings rightly tremble, so Jesus reassured his frightened disciples: 'don't be afraid' (v 20). Although not specifically termed a 'sign' in John's Gospel, walking on the water points to Jesus' power and authority: 'God placed all things under his feet'.[5]

Jesus has promised to be with us always but, in the absence of a visible, tangible presence, the storms of life that rise up against us in our faith journey can be confusing and frightening. It is reassuring to remember that when it feels as if we are in over our heads, the Lord who trod the waves underfoot has not lost control.

Create a tangible reminder of God's powerful presence – perhaps a line from a song or scripture verse as your screensaver – that can serve as encouragement in turbulent times.

---

[1] PJ Owens, 1829–1907, 'Will your anchor hold' [2] Exod 14:21; Josh 3:14–17; 2 Kings 2:8,14 [3] Job 9:8 [4] Exod 3:14 [5] Eph 1:22

BIBLE IN A YEAR: **2 Chronicles 35,36; Luke 1:39–80**

John 6:25–40

Better than Bread

Think about the difference between being a follower of Jesus and being a mere fan.

Crowds flocking to Jesus must have been a common sight in first-century Palestine, but merely *following after* does not make someone a *follower* of Jesus. People followed Jesus for a variety of reasons. We have already read that a great crowd followed him 'because they saw the signs he had performed by healing those who were ill' (v 2). After seeing – and tasting! – the miraculously multiplied loaves and fish, people's enthusiasm grew, until they were eager to seize this amazing bread-giver and 'make him king by force' (v 15). Although Jesus evaded the power-hungry crowd, they refused to give up and went looking for him by boat (v 24). Jesus, however, was not impressed by their persistence because he recognised the motives underlying their pursuit of him.

The crowd followed Jesus because they believed that they had found in him a never-ending supply of food – but Jesus yearned for them to believe in him as the source and substance of never-ending life (v 27). The miraculous provision of bread was a gift, intended as a sign pointing to the gracious and generous Giver of *all* good gifts, but, although these people eagerly sought God's gifts, they slighted the Giver by refusing to 'believe' in Jesus (vs 29,36). Jesus had not merely provided enough to take the edge off their hunger, he had let them have their fill (v 26); and now he longed to fill them with *himself*. The crowd, however, were hung up on the sign and failed to appreciate its significance. They were chasing after perishable food, whereas Jesus wanted them to pursue what was imperishable. They were focusing their efforts on what was temporary and transient, but Jesus invited them to set their hearts on what was eternal and enduring (v 27).

In Jesus, God invites you and me to feast on something far better than bread – he gives us himself, to be bread for our body, mind, heart and soul.

BIBLE IN A YEAR: **Ezra 1,2; Luke 2**

We Are What We Eat

Remember that when you 'thrill to God's Word' and 'chew on Scripture day and night', you are like 'a tree replanted in Eden, bearing fresh fruit every month'.[1]

Jesus proclaims that he is 'the bread of life' (v 48) and places his offer on the table – a feast of 'bread' straight from 'heaven' (v 41). This offer is open to all – 'anyone may eat and not die' (v 50, emphasis added). However, as the saying goes, 'You can lead a horse to water, but you can't make it drink!' Jesus invites us to his table where he himself is the feast, but he will never force-feed us. We have to choose to eat, drink and taste of his goodness and grace.

Food must be consumed before its benefits can be realised. Heaping our plates high accomplishes little unless we actually consume this food, digest it and absorb it into our bodies to nourish and strengthen us. The saying 'We are what we eat' is true! What we eat does not merely generate fuel for our bodies, it is also integrated into every cell in the body – skin, hair, blood, muscles and so on. What we eat affects not just our physical well-being but also our mental and emotional health.

In his discussion with the argumentative Jews, Jesus repeatedly emphasised the need to 'eat' (six times), 'drink' (three times), or 'feed' on him (twice), promising that 'whoever' feeds on him will enjoy a life-giving relationship with him for ever (vs 51–58). The expression 'to be consumed by' (or with) something (or someone) means to feel with such intensity that this affects all we do in every area of life. When we 'consume' Jesus, we allow ourselves to be consumed by him, assimilating his life into our own, absorbing and integrating his ways and values until they become an integral part of us, so that we can say, like Paul, 'I no longer live, but Christ lives in me.'[2]

'You're blessed when you've worked up a good appetite for God. He's food and drink in the best meal you'll ever eat.'[3]

[1] Ps 1:2,3, *The Message* [2] Gal 2:20 [3] Matt 5:6, *The Message*

BIBLE IN A YEAR: **Ezra 3,4; Luke 3**

FRIDAY 5 JULY
John 6:60–71

Be Led by the Lighthouse

Ponder Jesus' words: 'I am the light of the world. Whoever follows me will never walk in darkness, but will have the light of life.'[1]

Stephen Covey tells of a radio conversation between the captain of a battleship and a signalman.[2] Two ships seemed to be on a collision course… An argument takes place, with the signalman requesting the captain to adjust his course and the captain pulling rank and demanding that the signalman change course. The second 'ship' turns out to be a lighthouse! Naturally, the battleship must change course – or crash.

Many who claimed to be Jesus' disciples balked at his teachings: 'This is a hard teaching. Who can accept it?' (v 60). Despite their 'grumbling' (v 61), Jesus remained immoveable. It was not just that Jesus decided not to retract or dilute his words to make them more palatable, but also that he *could not*. His words, like that lighthouse, represent objective, unchanging, unalterable truth – words 'full of the Spirit and life' (v 63) – because Jesus himself *is* 'the truth'.[3] But while Jesus is unchanging, he challenges *us* to keep changing – constantly adjusting our course and fine-tuning our conduct by aligning ourselves with his truths and values. Just as a lighthouse enables ships to navigate through treacherous waters and reach safe harbour, Jesus seeks to direct and redirect us to himself. Nevertheless, he respects our free will. Many of those disgruntled disciples 'turned back and no longer followed him' (v 66), rejecting the life-giving bread from heaven and spurning his salvation (see yesterday's reading).

Even the Twelve, who had been hand-picked by Jesus, had to make a choice: 'You do not want to leave too, do you?' (v 67). Judas ultimately ignored the 'lighthouse' and chose a collision course (vs 64,70,71; see also John 13:30). But Peter wanted to be led by the lighthouse: 'Lord, to whom shall we go? You have the words of eternal life' (v 68).

Lord, shine your light into my life, and show me areas in which I must 'adjust' my course.

[1] John 8:12 [2] Stephen R. Covey, *The 7 Habits of Highly Effective People*, Simon & Schuster, 2004, p33
[3] John 14:6

BIBLE IN A YEAR: **Ezra 5,6; Psalm 77**

14

FREE MISSION SUPPORT

Scripture Union

Unlock the full potential of your outreach to children and young people with **FREE Mission Support** from Scripture Union.

· ·

Sign up today for inspiration and advice from experienced professionals:

su.org.uk/missionsupport

WE'D BE **GREAT** TOGETHER

Ezekiel 1–30

A DRAMATIC PROPHET

In 597 BC Nebuchadnezzar invaded Jerusalem, taking King Jehoiachin and most of the people into exile in Babylonia. Ezekiel, born into a priestly family, probably in 622 BC, was one of those taken to Babylon. There is no evidence that he ever returned to live in Jerusalem. In 587 BC the Babylonians returned, destroyed the Temple, executed King Zedekiah and exiled the remainder of the people. When Ezekiel was 30, the age at which he would have expected to start his priestly career in the Temple in Jerusalem, he was in exile in Babylonia. Suddenly and unexpectedly, God called him to be a prophet. He was married, but his wife died (ch 24). His ministry was to the exiles, a shattered and shell-shocked people suffering dislocation, loss and trauma, with all the attendant emotional and spiritual reactions.

That the book is written almost entirely as an autobiography strongly suggests that Ezekiel played a major part in the collection of prophetic words that bear his name. The book is unique among prophetic books of the Bible by being arranged in almost perfect chronological order, covering 593–571 BC. It is a book full of visions and repetition. Ezekiel's motto seemed to be 'Why say it once, if you can say it several times?' His prophecies are given in words and also expressed in mime and drama. The text is difficult, with some words and verses that have baffled translators.

He proclaims the holiness of God and the certainty of future judgement and disaster, begging his hearers to turn back to God from their sinful ways. Alongside this preaching of judgement, he is hard to equal among Old Testament prophets in declaring the amazing grace of God. While his actions and message may seem strange to the modern reader, there is much of his message which is relevant to us as we follow Jesus in 2024.

Stuart Weir

FOR FURTHER READING
Christopher Wright, *The Message of Ezekiel*, IVP, 2001

Wheels Within Wheels

'Holy, holy, holy is the Lord Almighty; the whole earth is full of his glory.'[1]

'As birthday treats go, Ezekiel's 30th birthday experience is unsurpassed.'[2] Ezekiel may have been thinking that he had reached the age when he should have been starting his service as a priest but, instead, he was in exile far from the Temple in Jerusalem. He may even, along with some of the exiles, have wondered, 'Has Israel's God been defeated by the Babylonian gods?' Rather than the heavens declaring the glory of God,[3] they seemed to proclaim his defeat.

It was the traditional Old Testament view that no one could see God and live, but prophets often had some kind of visionary experience of God to authenticate their ministry. All Ezekiel could bring himself to write about his vision was 'This was the appearance of the likeness of the glory of the LORD' (v 28). He was about to learn God's new mission for him.

Rather than wondering about the detail of the vision, or why Ezekiel's 'living creatures' (v 5) had only four wings while Isaiah's 'seraphim' had six,[4] we should concentrate on what the vision meant to Ezekiel. The description reads like an account by an eyewitness struggling to describe the indescribable – note phrases like 'The appearance of' (v 13), 'what looked something like' (v 22). The climax of his vision is the 'figure like that of a man' (v 26), on a throne, whom he describes as 'the likeness of the glory of the LORD' (v 28). Awestruck, Ezekiel realises that the figure is none other than God! God is right here with him by the river Kebar. God is still on the throne, reigning in power.

We too have seen the glory of God, not in a vision but in a man – the man Jesus. Reflect on the wonder of Immanuel, God with us.

---

[1] Isa 6:3 [2] Christopher Wright, *The Message of Ezekiel*, IVP, 2001, p43 [3] Ps 19:1 [4] Isa 6:2

BIBLE IN A YEAR: **Ezra 7,8; Luke 4**

Psalm 143

Only by Grace

'Other refuge have I none, / hangs my helpless soul on thee'.[1]

This psalm is a song of lament by a man oppressed by enemies. Paralysed by fear, deeply depressed and close to despair, he prays. Traditionally such prayers were offered in the evening, with the expectation that God's answer would come in the morning (v 8). The psalmist recognises that he cannot approach God with any sense of entitlement based on his own merits. His appeal for help is founded on God's name, character and 'unfailing love' (v 12). He knows all about grace! Moreover, he knows the problem is not his alone, as he acknowledges that 'no one living is righteous before [God]' (v 2), a phase reminiscent of Paul's 'no one will be declared righteous in God's sight by the works of the law'.[2]

We may be uncomfortable with the psalmist's desire in the final verse to see all his enemies annihilated, but he is praying 'in line with the Old Testament covenant tradition according to which blessings and curses for the obedient and disobedient, respectively, are equally real'.[3] Today, of course, we have the benefit of understanding God through Christ, who has taken our judgement on himself.

There is much here that would have resonated with Ezekiel, such as 'in your righteousness, bring me out of trouble' (v 11). Ezekiel had experienced the enemy pursuing and crushing him in the Babylonian conquest of Jerusalem (v 3). Ezekiel would have been mindful of all God's past interventions for his covenant people (v 5), but would have tempered that encouragement with his recognition of the sins of the people, which had led to the exile. Ezekiel's strong faith in a God of faithfulness, righteousness and unfailing love echoes the psalmist's, but perhaps would not have asked God not to hide his face (v 7), following the vision of chapter 1!

Pray for frightened people in war zones, who share the psalmist's conviction that only God can save them.

---

[1] Charles Wesley, 1707–88, 'Jesus, lover of my soul' [2] Rom 3:20 [3] AA Anderson, *The Book of Psalms*, Volume 2, Bloomsbury, 1981, p930

BIBLE IN A YEAR: **Ezra 9,10; Luke 5**

Blood, Toil and Tears

Thank you, Lord, that when you call us to do difficult things, you equip us and go with us.

While he is still reeling from the experience of the vision, Ezekiel is called in to a job interview. He receives his prophetic commission. He is to be God's messenger to the exiles in Babylonia. Thorns and scorpions (2:6) comprise a powerful metaphor for what the job entailed: presenting God's message to people who will not listen! With his propensity for repetition, Ezekiel records, five times, that the people are rebellious. The good news is that he is being sent to his own people; the bad news is that foreigners would have been more open to the message. He will discover that 'A prophet is not without honour except in his own town'.[1]

He is commanded to eat the scroll, meaning that he must internalise the message before communicating it to others. In contrast to the call of Moses, Isaiah and Jeremiah, we hear no word of response from Ezekiel – perhaps it would have been rude for him to speak with his mouth full![2] We might have expected the encounter to have ended with Ezekiel portrayed as a holy man of God emboldened by his amazing calling by God. It is therefore a shock to read that his demeanour was 'bitterness' and 'anger' (3:14).

Was the reason for this reaction his anger with God for being given this appalling task? It was bad enough to be in exile suffering the living death of the refugee and to have lost his career as a priest, without having to endure the unpopularity and social exclusion that his prophetic ministry would bring. Only the strong hand of the Lord upheld him and restrained these emotions.

God has spoken dramatically to us through Jesus the Word, full of truth.[3] We, like Ezekiel, are called to share the message with others.

[1] Matt 13:57 [2] C Wright, 2001, p60 [3] John 1:14

BIBLE IN A YEAR: **Nehemiah 1,2; Psalm 78:1–37**

Ezekiel 3:16–27

The Watchman

Thank you, Lord, that you call us to serve you. Open our ears to hear your message clearly and help us to be ready to obey.

We next encounter Ezekiel the would-be-priest and would-rather-not-be-prophet seven days later. If Ezekiel had spent the week in silent, angry resistance, it is overcome by another encounter with God's glory. This time there is no 'appearance of the likeness'.[1] He knows instantly that this *is* the 'glory of the LORD' (v 23).

The end of the chapter is problematic. Why should God tell Ezekiel he was to warn the Israelites, then commission him as a watchman before he was told to go and shut himself in his house and remain silent? Perhaps he was commanded to be silent except when God gave him something explicit to say. Perhaps, like Jeremiah, who remained in Jerusalem, he would be imprisoned and stopped from prophesying.

The main point of the passage is the interpretation of his mission in terms of being a watchman. He is addressed as 'son of man' (vs 17,25) – an expression used 90 times in the book, simply meaning 'human'. We should not read any Messianic meaning into it. The image of watchmen was common among the prophets.[2] The metaphor of the prophet as a watchman is vivid. A sentry posted in a tower watching for any movement of the enemy would be responsible for alerting the people. A watchman who fails to give warning of approaching danger is personally responsible for the ensuing disaster. The task of the watchman is not to formulate battle plans or coordinate the defence but only to stay awake, to see what is coming and sound the alarm. The analogy breaks down somewhat in this case, because God is the enemy of *sinful* Israel, yet it is God who sets the sentry to warn them. This is a picture of the tension between grace and judgement in the heart of God.

How can we take our responsibility to be watchmen more seriously, warning a lost generation in our community of their need of Christ?

[1] Ezek 1:28 [2] Isa 56:10; Jer 6:17; Hos 9:8; Hab 2:1

BIBLE IN A YEAR: **Nehemiah 3,4; Luke 6**

A Dramatic Siege

'Lord Jesus Christ, Wisdom, dwell in our hearts, we pray, by your most Holy Spirit, that out of the abundance of our hearts, our mouths may speak your praise.'[1]

Imagine going to visit your pastor and finding them lying on their side in front of their house! It was, however, quite common for Old Testament prophets to portray their message in dramatic forms or acted parables.[2] It seems unlikely that Ezekiel lay for the entire period, morning to night, but rather only during the hours when he was acting as a prophet. After all, there's no point in doing a drama if no one is watching. In the close-knit community of the exiles, word would surely have got around that Ezekiel was at it again. It would have been a shock to the exiles that Ezekiel portrayed God as the enemy of Jerusalem, not its defender. The point of the drama is to warn the exiles not to place their hopes in the survival of Jerusalem and to show them the starvation rations the people of Jerusalem would have to survive on while under Babylonian siege. While Ezekiel could accept calmly the limitations on his diet, he drew the line at cooking with human excrement.

It must have been difficult to be a prophet's wife. Imagine watching your husband, starving himself, making an exhibition of himself, possibly borrowing household items as props for his work. In a low-budget production, Ezekiel starts off playing the role of God attacking Jerusalem but then changes in verse 4, now taking the part of his own people and, in words reminiscent of Isaiah 53, bearing their sins.

Note: As the next oracle in 8:1 is dated just 13 months later, it is generally thought that Ezekiel did his 390 and 40 days (vs 5,6) simultaneously rather than consecutively.

Ezekiel suffered for his people and will suffer with them. How much do we empathise with those around us who suffer?

[1] Christina Rossetti, 1830–94 [2] See Isa 20; Jer 13 – and Agabus in Acts 21

BIBLE IN A YEAR: **Nehemiah 5,6; Luke 7**

Ezekiel 5

Bad Hair Day

**'Father I want to trust in Jesus. I want to give my life to him, Lord.
I want to exemplify the love Jesus has for the world.'[1]**

After 13 months of eating starvation rations and lying down, Ezekiel moves seamlessly into another astonishing drama. Cutting off presumably a year's growth of hair would have been a challenging task. Where would he have found a sword? Did he use one of his wife's kitchen knives? Presumably word would have spread that Ezekiel was up to something and a crowd would have gathered to watch. Shaving his head, often seen as an act of mourning or disgrace and shame, would have been stressful enough, but more so for Ezekiel as priests were expressly forbidden from shaving their heads.[2] His drama is what Wright calls 'a one man double act',[3] in which he represents the Lord wielding the sword in judgement, but his hair, representing Israel, is the recipient of the judgement. When God says (v 11), 'I myself will shave you', this recalls Isaiah's reference to God using the king of Assyria to shave the people.[4]

Ezekiel then explains the drama with words, stating that Jerusalem, which should have been the centre of the nations and indeed a light to the nations, shockingly is morally worse than the pagan nations around it. In verse 12, Ezekiel delivers the word of the Sovereign Lord, explaining the dividing of his hair in terms of a prophecy of death, plague, famine and exile when Jerusalem falls to the Babylonians. For Israelites expecting, as God's chosen people, that God would protect them, the words in verse 8, 'I myself am against you', would have been shocking words to hear.

In case we are reading this chapter smugly, as New Testament Christians, we need to remember that Paul castigated the Corinthians for sins 'that even pagans do not tolerate'.[5] Sin among God's people is worse in God's sight than among non-believers.

How effectively do you think the church today represents God to society around us? What could we do better?

---

[1] https://graceandprayers.com/ [2] Lev 21:5 [3] C Wright, 2001. p83 [4] Isa 7:20 [5] 1 Cor 5:1

BIBLE IN A YEAR: **Nehemiah 7,8; Luke 8**

Adulterous Hearts

Thank God that his mercy is never far behind his judgement.

After prophesying the doom of Jerusalem, Ezekiel now addresses the whole land of Israel. Of course, God is not angry with the mountains; it is just that the hills were the site of the high places where so much idol worship was practised. The tragedy is that King Josiah had abolished the high places[1] but within 30 years of his death the old pagan practices had returned.

In referring to idol worshippers as having 'adulterous hearts' (v 9), Ezekiel is following in the footsteps of other prophets before him, recognising idolatry as unfaithfulness to Israel's covenant relationship with God. Even some of those who had not totally forsaken God may have hedged their bets, by worshipping God but also keeping on good terms with the local gods as an extra insurance. Ezekiel was forceful in his condemnation of the worship of idols, by his use, 38 times, of an unusual and therefore arresting Hebrew word for idol – *gillulim*,[2] a word rarely used outside this book.

The clapping and stamping of verse 11 (a Hebrew triumph-song) celebrate God's triumph over the wicked. This is followed by a familiar message of judgement by sword, plague and famine. While the words may seem harsh, the prophet is simply repeating the message of Leviticus 26, familiar to him from his priestly training, with its warnings against idol worship. He speaks also of the promise of peace and prosperity if the people obey God's commands. Four times Ezekiel explains the nature and purpose of God's judgement (vs 7,10,13,14). Despite the violent language used to describe it, God's judgement is not vindictive retribution but merciful restoration so that 'you will know that I am the LORD' (v 7), words which express Ezekiel's longing that all people will come and worship God.

How do you respond to the often angry and violent descriptions of God's judgement? How would you describe the nature and purpose of his judgement?

[1] 2 Kings 23:13   [2] JB Taylor, *Ezekiel*, IVP, 1969, p91

BIBLE IN A YEAR: **Nehemiah 9,10; Psalm 78:38–72**

Ezekiel 7

The End is Nigh

Thank you, Lord, that you are a God who speaks. Help me today to hear your word to me and to respond.

This is not an easy chapter to understand, not least because it is poetry. Some phrases have baffled translators. One commentator called the chapter 'a hotchpotch of irony and wordplay'.[1] However, the basic message is clear: God's patience is finally exhausted. Just as Amos warned the northern kingdom of Israel, 'The time is ripe for my people Israel',[2] so Ezekiel warns Judah that time has run out. This message is introduced as early as verse 2 with 'The end! The end has come'. The message is repeated in verses 3 and 6, then confirmed by references to the day (v 10), the time and the day (vs 7,12) and the 'day of the LORD's wrath' (v 19) – not to mention the prediction of doom and disaster (vs 24–27).

Ezekiel's graphic description of the impending disaster includes words familiar from earlier chapters – the sword, plague and famine – and also references to economic calamity, against which wealth is no defence. The prophet also warns that the usual sources of wisdom and help will be useless, as prophets, priests, elders and even the king will be powerless in the wake of terror, calamity and disaster. The justice of God's actions is stressed and repeated: 'I will judge you according to your conduct' (vs 3,4,8,9,27).

The final verse of the chapter includes Ezekiel's signature, 'Then they will know that I am the LORD', showing again Ezekiel's belief that the ultimate purpose of God's judgement is not revenge or punishment for its own sake but a desire that the people should acknowledge their sin and turn back to God. The chapter paints a grim picture of the disaster that would come in 587 BC. We must also recognise that God would not have been just if he had not acted in response to the evil practices of his people.

What sins and practices among God's people would alarm a modern-day Ezekiel?

[1] JB Taylor, 1969, p94 [2] Amos 8:2

BIBLE IN A YEAR: **Nehemiah 11,12; Luke 9**

Psalm 144

King and Country

Lord Jesus, who set us an example of meekness and majesty, help us to imitate your humility.

The king praises God on behalf of the nation. The psalm, as we have it, was probably put together in the period before the fall of Jerusalem in Ezekiel's time, with almost all the content repeated from earlier psalms – what Anderson calls 'a mosaic of various fragments of other psalms'.[1] The psalm opens with an acknowledgement of who God is and what he has done, causing the psalmist first to turn to prayer for God's intervention (vs 5–8) and then to break out in song (v 9–11), before ending with a reflection looking beyond the present to a time of future prosperity. The intervention he requests is a full-on theophany (v 5), a 'breaking into time and space of a colossal eternal energy with devastating effect'.[2]

The psalmist may be a king, but he is struck by his own mortality and insignificance in comparison with God. He raises a great philosophical question:

why should God, who is eternal – always has been and always will be – take note of humans whose lives, in comparison, are but a breath or a fleeting shadow? In another psalm the writer marvelled in similar fashion that God had made humanity 'a little lower than the angels and crowned them with glory and honour'.[3] Paul, too, recognised that, as humans, 'we have this treasure in jars of clay to show that this all-surpassing power is from God and not from us'.[4]

Prosperity in Old Testament times was seen as a blessing from God, so it is normal for the psalmist, having prayed for God's intervention to deliver the people from their enemies, to anticipate the outcome in terms of economic and social blessing. Yet he finished with a clear acknowledgement of the source of their blessings and of how favoured they were to be the recipients.

In our sophisticated society and our greater understanding of how the universe works, how can we maintain a humble and thankful spirit?

[1] AA Anderson, 1981, p931 [2] Leslie Allen, 'Psalms', in *A Bible Commentary for Today*, P&I, 1979, p698 [3] Ps 8:5 [4] 2 Cor 4:7

BIBLE IN A YEAR: **Nehemiah 13; Luke 10**

Ezekiel 8,9

'I am a Jealous God'[1]

Help us to see our sin as you see it. Help us to acknowledge our failures and seek forgiveness instead of trying to justify ourselves.

The elders of Judah, in Babylonia, come to see Ezekiel, but he pops off to Jerusalem, a thousand miles away! Recording the date represented proof that he had predicted the event in advance. We cannot be certain exactly what happened, but Ezekiel probably remained physically present with the elders. A prophet being in two places simultaneously has a parallel with Elisha.[2]

The vision reveals to Ezekiel that pagan practices were rife in the Temple in Jerusalem. He sees the glory of the Lord move to the threshold of the Temple (9:3), offended by the sin of Israel. The purpose of the vision may have been to show Ezekiel the reasons for the destruction he was to proclaim and to help him rebut the arguments that God was being unfair. Ezekiel intercedes on behalf of the people (9:8), in the prophetic tradition of Moses, Jeremiah and Amos.[3] Ezekiel is not just concerned for the people: he had a passion for the glory and purposes of God in the world. The terrible truth of this chapter is that not only are God's people not immune from God's judgement but they will be judged more harshly because of the opportunities they have been given.

The statement that judgement is to 'begin at my sanctuary' (see 9:6) should send a shiver down our spines. Remember Peter's warning that it is time for judgement to begin with God's household.[4] As we look around the Christian world, we see historical sexual abuse scandals, the breakdown of Christian marriages, infidelity, trust in money and possessions, church politics, factions, corruption and power games: 'just a sample of the temptations to idolatry that surround us and entice us away from the integrity of a fully biblical faith in the one living God and in the sole lordship of Jesus Christ'.[5]

Do we as individuals and as church need to take God's judgement more seriously?

[1] see Exod 20:5 [2] 2 Kings 5:26 [3] Num 14:13–19; Amos 7:2,5; Jer 14:19–21 [4] 1 Pet 4:17
[5] C Wright, 2001. p109

BIBLE IN A YEAR: **Esther 1–3; Psalm 79**

God's Glory Departs

'The Word became flesh and made his dwelling among us. We have seen his glory, the glory of the one and only Son'.[1]

Ezekiel had seen the people of Jerusalem put to the sword. Then he saw the city itself set on fire. The main point of the chapter is that God's glory leaves the Temple, because the glory of God cannot continue to dwell in the city that God is handing over to the fires of judgement. We don't know quite what Ezekiel meant by 'the glory of God'. As Christians, we are blessed to have seen the glory of God, the radiance of his essential nature, reflected in Jesus Christ.

Much of Ezekiel's vision in chapter 1 is repeated and clarified. Ezekiel identifies the living creatures as cherubim, who had a role of protection in the Garden of Eden,[2] in the Temple[3] and in worship.[4] Here, by horrifying contrast, their function includes judgement. Ezekiel discovers the purpose of the fiery, flaming heart of the throne chariot: it is to provide fire for the final destruction of the city after the killing of the inhabitants. The man clothed in linen is to scatter burning coals like incendiary bombs around the city. The account recalls the destruction of Sodom and Gomorrah. The historical fulfilment of this vision is recorded by Jeremiah.[5]

The glory of the presence of the Lord, which first left the holy of holies for the threshold of the Temple, then settled on the chariot throne. Seeing the glory of God disappearing from the Temple would have been devastating for Ezekiel, the priest, exiled and powerless, particularly if, as the text seems to imply, he was the only one to see it.

Temple activities continued after the Lord's presence had departed. How do we ensure that our corporate worship is more about the presence of the Lord than the music and performance?

[1] John 1:14 [2] Gen 3:24 [3] Ezek 41:17–20 [4] Exod 25:18–22 [5] Jer 52:12,13

BIBLE IN A YEAR: **Esther 4,5; Luke 11**

Ezekiel 11

A New Heart

'O for a heart to praise my God, / a heart from sin set free, / a heart that always feels thy blood / so freely shed for me.'[1]

Ezekiel is given two messages, one for the people of Jerusalem and the other for the exiles. Then, suddenly, he comes out of his trance and is fully back with the elders of Judah.[2] Quite what they made of Ezekiel's visions, if he indeed shared these with them, we are not told. There is a certain irony that Ezekiel sees the 25 men (v 1) at the gate of the city, precisely the place where God departed from the city – but they had not noticed it. Ezekiel's message to the 25 is in the form of a strange image of meat in a pot, the meaning of which is not entirely clear. The most likely interpretation is that those who had stayed in Jerusalem saw themselves as the choice pieces of meat being cooked in a pot, protected by the pot. The bones and offal outside the pot were the unprotected riff-raff, who had been taken into exile. When Pelatiah drops down dead – rather like Ananias and Sapphira in Acts 5 – Ezekiel is shaken and starts to pray that God would not completely destroy his people.

God's answer is a promise of hope and restoration which would come not in Jerusalem but through the exiles, reinforcing the message we find elsewhere in the book that God can be present with his people anywhere, not just in Jerusalem and the Temple. In a passage similar to Jeremiah's prophecy,[3] God promises to put a new heart and a new spirit in his people, who will be restored once again in the covenant relationship to be God's people. The promise is, however, immediately followed by a warning of judgement on those who refuse to turn from their idols to the Lord. They will miss out on the opportunity of a heart transplant.

'Above all else, guard your heart, for everything you do flows from it.'[4] How do we guard our heart?

[1] Charles Wesley 1707–1788 [2] Cf Ezek 8:1 [3] Jer 31:31–34 [4] Prov 4:23

BIBLE IN A YEAR: **Esther 6,7; Luke 12**

A Rebellious People

'Who is like you, LORD God Almighty? You, LORD, are mighty, and your faithfulness surrounds you.'[1]

Ezekiel is to perform two more symbolic actions to communicate God's word to the exiles. One may wonder again what Ezekiel's wife thought as she watched her husband making a hole in the wall of their house and crawling through it!

In chapter 4 Ezekiel is to eat siege rations. Now he is to eat with fear and trembling, symbolising the fear of those awaiting the destruction of the city (vs 17,18). He is only to take with him what he can carry on a long walk. This dramatises an attempt to escape from the enemy under cover of darkness rather than a people being led into exile. The fulfilment of the prophecy is explained in verses 12 and 13, when the prince's – King Zedekiah's – escape attempt fails and he 'will not see' because he is blinded by the Babylonians.[2] However, Ezekiel's words show clearly that it is not just the Babylonian army that is against the king, but also the arm of the Lord.

The bottom line of this chapter and of every chapter of Ezekiel is not the detail of what is happening or will happen, but its theological purpose, which is stated in verse 15 and repeated in 16: 'they will know that I am the LORD'. As Taylor writes: 'What men fail to appreciate in prosperity, they will occasionally learn through adversity'.[3] One of the objections from Ezekiel's hearers is basically 'you keep prophesying but nothing ever happens' (see v 22). Jeremiah would probably have added that that was the story of his life, with 40 years of prophecy being dismissed by the people. As modern Christians are we in danger of not really believing, for example, the second coming of Christ because, despite 2,000 years of promises, it has still not happened?

Ezekiel was resolute in his consistent proclamation of an unpopular message. In what ways are we tempted to water down God's message to make it more acceptable to our generation?

[1] Ps 89:8 [2] Jer 52:8–11 [3] JB Taylor, 1969, p116

BIBLE IN A YEAR: **Esther 8–10; Luke 13**

Ezekiel 13

True or False?

'Be still, and know that I am God; I will be exalted among the nations, I will be exalted in the earth.'[1]

One reason for the people's unwillingness to believe Ezekiel's warnings was that false prophets were telling them that everything was going to be fine. It is a recurring theme in Ezekiel and Jeremiah: they had not only to proclaim God's message but also to call out the false prophets. Here Ezekiel compares them to jackals digging under the city wall and undermining it (v 4) and likens their message (vs 10–12) to someone building a flimsy wall and saying that it wouldn't fall down after it had been whitewashed. The basis for Ezekiel's denunciation of the false prophets is that they are self-commissioned, not called by God; they speak out of their own minds, not the word of God, and they follow their own spirit instead of the spirit of God. He pronounces God's judgement on them, 'I am against you' (v 8), adding that they have no place in the true Israel of God. In contrast, Ezekiel has seen a vision of God and has received a message from God.

There is strong denunciation of a group of women prophets, who seem to be using witchcraft and sorcery – magic wrist bands and veils – perhaps a Babylonian influence because there such practices were common. They clearly had people under their spell, literally. It may have been a kind of protection racket. In contrast to the condemnation of the prophets, the women seem to get off quite lightly, suffering only the loss of their influence and livelihood.

The overall message of the chapter fits into Ezekiel's message to the exiles that God's judgement is coming and that any prophecies of good times ahead and promises of peace come from a prophet's own head and are not a message from God. When God acts in fulfilment of prophecy, 'Then you will know that I am the LORD' (vs 9,14,23).

At times we are deceived by false prophets and preachers. How do we discern truth from false teaching?

[1] Ps 46:10

BIBLE IN A YEAR: **Job 1,2; Psalm 80**

No Proxy Salvation

'... you are to give him the name Jesus, because he will save his people from their sins.'[1]

The elders who came to Ezekiel were guilty of idolatry, which is condemned throughout the Bible.[2] The idea of God enticing a prophet and then holding him guilty (vs 9,10) is difficult. While we may recall God hardening Pharaoh's heart[3] or the lying spirit sent by divine permission to mislead Ahab's prophets,[4] such episodes have to be balanced by and interpreted in the light of statements like 'God cannot be tempted by evil, nor does he tempt anyone'.[5] Ezekiel, with his Old Testament perspective, would have seen God's intervention in national life in a different way from most twenty-first-century Christians. As New Testament Christians, we can see a fuller picture.

Based on the belief that their God would not act in judgement against his own people, the elders may have argued that the community would be saved on account of a righteous few, citing Abraham's successful intercession for Sodom and Gomorrah[6] or Noah's righteousness saving his family.[7] The elders are told in no uncertain terms that Jerusalem's plight is now so desperate that even the presence of the most righteous men who ever lived could not save it from judgement. We need to remember, however, that the purpose of divine judgement here is the re-establishment of the covenant between God and the people (v 11).

The idea of the unrighteous being saved by the righteous is at the heart of the Christian gospel. The angel's message to Joseph was that Jesus would 'save his people from their sins',[8] repeated later in the Gospel in the statement that the Son of Man came 'to give his life as a ransom for many'.[9] We can be thankful that Jesus came, not as judge, but as our Saviour.

None of us has a physical idol in our home – but what kind of idols are we tempted to set up in our heart?

---

[1] Matt 1:21 [2] Eg Lev 26:1 [3] Eg Exod 4:21 [4] 1 Kings 22:20–23 [5] James 1:13 [6] Gen 18:16–33 [7] Gen 6:8,9
[8] Matt 1:21 [9] Matt 20:28

BIBLE IN A YEAR: **Job 3,4; Luke 14**

Psalm 145

Grace

'Dear Lord, I praise you and I love being in your presence. Thank you for the sacrifice you made for me on the cross.'[1]

This is a Hebrew acrostic psalm: each verse begins with a successive letter of the Hebrew alphabet. This may constrain the flow of the poem but it keeps the psalm (covering an infinite subject – God's character) to a reasonable length.[2] AA Anderson suggests that we should imagine a worship leader singing the song, with the congregation joining in a chorus like 'Blessed be God's name for ever'.[3] Because of the reference to provision of food (v 15), the Jewish community sang the psalm as a harvest anthem, while the ancient church sang it as a lunch-time grace. Anderson notes that there was a tradition among pious Jews to recite this psalm three times daily in the synagogue![4] Dramatically, the psalmist speaks to, and about, the Lord, so that the poem seamlessly blends personal prayer and corporate praise.

One of the key Scriptural descriptions of God comes in verse 8, also recorded in three other places.[5] The concept of God's love was often proclaimed only to the community of God's people in relation to the covenant, but there is a universalist theme to this psalm. The following verses show that God's grace is for 'all', a word used 16 times in the psalm. Alongside God's mighty acts, we see the tenderness and intimacy of the compassion with which he loves his creatures.

As we have observed, there are always two sides to Ezekiel's prophecies, blessing and judgement. Punishing the wicked is a responsibility of the Sovereign God. Those who respond positively to God are rewarded with his presence and blessing. As Ellison puts it, 'The wicked reap what they have desired – absence from God.'[6] Overall, we should see the psalm as a glorious expression of joyful, exultant worship. Great is the Lord! He is most worthy of praise.

Read the psalm aloud three times as an act of worship.

---

[1] biblestudytools.com [2] HL Ellison, *Psalms*, SU, 1967, p121 [3] AA Anderson, 1981, p936
[4] AA Anderson, 1981, p937 [5] Ps 86:15; 103:8; Exod 34:6 [6] HL Ellison, 1967, p121

BIBLE IN A YEAR: **Job 5,6; Luke 15**

No Beanstalk

Thank you, Jesus, for your words: 'I am the true vine, and my Father is the gardener'.[1]

Comparing Israel to a vine has a long history in Hebrew tradition, going back to Genesis.[2] It is an obvious image, as vines are such a key element in Palestinian agriculture. The image is also used in the New Testament.[3] The psalmist compares Israel to a vine that God rescued from Egypt and planted in its own land, growing to such an extent that the mountains were in its shade and its roots reached the sea[4] – 'no ordinary vine, this was the Jack and the Beanstalk kind of vine'.[5]

Ezekiel loves metaphors; chapters 15–23 are full of them. However, Ezekiel's metaphors are rarely pleasant. He often tends to subvert familiar positive images (for example the bride who turns whore in chapter 16, and the ship becoming a wreck in chapter 27). This subversion led to the accusation that he spoke 'in parables'.[6] Here, in chapter 15, Ezekiel

turns the familiar vine metaphor on its head by diverting attention from grapes and wine to the wood. The image here is of vine wood, notoriously useless for making things and even more useless in its charred state. The application is to Jerusalem, insignificant and useless compared with the superpowers around – and of even less value after being charred – a reference to the partial destruction of Jerusalem in the invasion of 597 BC. The city is good for nothing other than being thrown back into the fire, a prophetic prediction of the destruction to come in 587 BC.

It is hard to overestimate the shock of the hearers, as this subversion of the familiar image of Israel as God's flourishing vine shows them how God sees them – so that the total destruction of Jerusalem and its inhabitants is the inevitable outcome.

Against what kind of issues in our society would the Lord set his face?

[1] John 15:1 [2] Gen 49:22 [3] Mark 12:1–9; John 15:1–8 [4] Ps 80:8–11 [5] Nancy Bowen, *Ezekiel*, Abingdon Press, 2010, p82 [6] Ezek 20:49

BIBLE IN A YEAR: **Job 7,8; Psalms 81,82**

Ezekiel 16:1–34

Warning: Offensive Content!

'Nothing in my hand I bring, / simply to thy cross I cling; / naked, come to thee for dress'.[1]

This chapter is not likely to be preached from or read aloud in church! The delinquency of Jerusalem is portrayed in a powerful and revolting allegory. The city is compared to a baby girl exposed at birth without the normal minimum of attention. God takes pity on her, cares for her and brings her up, making her his bride with garments and ornaments fit for a queen. Instead of showing gratitude and fidelity, however, she turns to prostitution and commits fornication with strangers – Egyptians, Assyrians, Chaldeans – even bribing them to become her lovers. The language borders on vulgarity. Not for the first time, one may wonder what Ezekiel's wife was thinking as she heard it!

Ezekiel is deliberately using shock tactics to show the people how they have utterly and repeatedly rejected God. His use of graphic imagery may have been influenced by Hosea who, 150 years earlier, drew on the experiences of his own wife's unfaithfulness. Hosea expressed the relationship between God and his people in terms of the covenant of marriage in order to demonstrate Israel's spiritual adultery. Ezekiel is attacking the view, generated by their history, that God would always defend Israel and that Jerusalem was inviolate because of the covenant. Ezekiel's ultimate purpose is to make the exiles recognise the truth about the situation and thus drive them to genuine repentance.

This is an uncomfortable passage, even implying that Israel's sin included the abhorrent child sacrifice to pagan idols. It includes, however, a moving and powerful description of God, who chose Israel for his own purpose among the nations because of his own mysterious love and grace, not because of any attribute they possessed. Just like us. We need to take from this a fresh assurance of God's grace and mercy.

The image of marriage in the Old Testament is developed in the New Testament. What does it mean to you that the church is the bride of Christ?

[1] Augustus Toplady, 1740–78, 'Rock of Ages'

BIBLE IN A YEAR: **Job 9,10; Luke 16**

More Shock Tactics

'I, even I, am he who blots out your transgressions, for my own sake, and remembers your sins no more.'[1]

The unpleasant description continues 'from one degree of gory to another'.[2] We need to remember that the portrayal is allegorical and symbolic. There is no suggestion that God actually behaved like this, nor should the story be seen as sanctioning such behaviour among humans. We must also be careful not to approach this passage with modern eyes and read modern agendas into it. Nor should we be put off by the way the story loads all the guilt and wickedness on the female character while portraying in a more positive light the husband, who is abusive: stripping, humiliating and allowing the violent assault of his wife. Similarly, we must not judge the practice of capital punishment for adultery (v 40) by modern standards. Such objections, though valid, are irrelevant to the point that Ezekiel was making to an ancient people, couching his words in culturally relevant terms. His main point is that while God will judge on the basis of what the nations deserve, he will also extend grace.

Amidst this difficult chapter, we find an encouraging promise in verses 59 and 60 that God will remember his covenant with his people and indeed will replace it with an everlasting covenant through Jesus. Verse 63 also reminds us of a point that we may often forget. When God forgives people's sins, he 'will remember their sins no more'.[3] The sinner may find them harder to forget! Paul, for example, always remembered that he had persecuted the church. The value of such memory is to keep us from pride and remind us, as forgiven sinners, that we have a past of which to be ashamed and that our justification is all through God's grace.[4]

The allegorical representation of Samaria and Jerusalem as Oholah and Oholibah is developed in chapter 23.

The sin of Sodom (v 49) is that 'they did not help the poor and needy'. How would Ezekiel assess your church in that area?

---

[1] Isa 43:25   [2] C Wright, 2001, p144   [3] Jer 31:34   [4] JB Taylor, 1969, p142

BIBLE IN A YEAR: **Job 11,12; Luke 17**

A Messianic Oracle

'Hail to the Lord's Anointed, / great David's greater Son! /
Hail in the time appointed, / his reign on earth begun!'[1]

This chapter is in three parts – a riddle, an explanation of the riddle and a positive promise. Riddles – rather like Aesop's fables[2] – were common in the ancient world: for example, Samson's riddle to the Philistines.[3] In Ezekiel's riddle (also called an allegory and a parable in some translations), the eagles behave anthropomorphically and we, along with those who listened to him, are drawn dramatically and prophetically into actual events in their world – the vacillating policy of Zedekiah which led to his downfall. The great eagle is Nebuchadnezzar. Lebanon, known for its cedar trees used in building Jerusalem, represents Jerusalem. The top shoot broken off is King Jehoiachin who was carried into exile in 597 BC to Babylon, a city of traders. The seedling (v 5) is Zedekiah, whom Nebuchadnezzar appointed to govern. The 'low, spreading vine' (v 6) refers to the lowly status of Zedekiah as a puppet king. The second great eagle is Pharaoh, who enticed Zedekiah from his allegiance to Nebuchadnezzar, promising him protection but ultimately failing to save him. The themes of submission, infidelity and their consequences link this chapter to the previous one.

The final three verses pick up the language of the allegory. Here it is not the eagle but God himself who breaks off the shoot which grows into a splendid cedar, the promised Messiah from the house of David.[4] Ezekiel looks forward to a day when all the trees of the forest – all nations of the world – will recognise God's authority. Ultimately, the security and fruitfulness of Israel will come, not from either of the two eagles, but from God himself. When God intervenes to reverse the fortunes of his people, the world will know who has done it.

Zedekiah put his trust in Pharaoh rather than in God. In whom or what are we tempted to trust rather than in God?

[1] James Montgomery, 1771–1854 [2] N Bowen, 2010, p94 [3] Judg 14:14 [4] Ezek 34:23; 37:24; Jer 23:5

BIBLE IN A YEAR: **Job 13,14; Luke 18**

It's Not Fair!

'We pray, Lord, that you will right all the wrongs that are taking place in our world and vindicate those that are being treated unjustly.'[1]

The proverb quoted in verse 2, 'The parents eat sour grapes, and the children's teeth are set on edge' was very familiar to Ezekiel's contemporaries. It is also quoted and refuted by Jeremiah.[2] It was, however, not entirely untrue: indeed, the basis of much of Ezekiel's own teaching was that the sufferings of the exile could be traced back to the persistent rebellion, idolatry and unfaithfulness to the covenant by previous generations. The problem was that for the exiles it had 'led to a spirit of fatalism and irresponsibility',[3] a belief in karma or an ancient expression of 'it is what it is'. If the exiles could convince themselves that God was being unfair, they could claim to be victims rather than sinners and get themselves off the hook. Ezekiel is maintaining that each generation is responsible for its own actions.

By using his priestly training, Ezekiel sets out three case studies to make his point. It is interesting that, despite being a priest, he did not define righteousness exclusively, or even predominantly, in ritual terms, but rather he 'ranges from the religious rituals, through private and intimate sexual behaviour, to the public arena of social, economic and judicial activity'.[4]

Ezekiel ends his reflection on the relationship between God's justice and man's freedom with a call to repent, emphasising God's eagerness to pardon. God longs for us to see our need of him. His passion for his people is apparent in the final exclamation, 'I take no pleasure in the death of anyone ... Repent and live!' (v 32).

In what ways are we tempted to blame circumstances and society rather than take responsibility for our own sins?

[1] www.xavier.edu/jesuitresource/online-resources/prayer-index/justice-prayers [2] Jer 31:29 [3] JB Taylor, 1969, p147 [4] C Wright, 2001, p194

BIBLE IN A YEAR: **Job 15–17; Psalms 83,84**

A Lament for Judah

'I call to you, O Lord, and all I get is your answering machine! We take our cries directly to the top. God, however, seems very far away.'[1]

The disasters that befell the kings of Judah are described in terms of the misfortunes of a brood of lion cubs. The first part of the chapter is an extended metaphor and the second a simile within the genre of lamentation, giving the reader a further example of Ezekiel's poetic gift. Most translations set this chapter out as poetry in what is known as lamentation metre – as used, for example, in the book of Lamentations – composed in distinctive mournful tones with a rhythm that is almost impossible to reproduce in an English translation. Chapter 18 ended with the words 'Repent and live', so it is ironic that chapter 19 starts with a funeral dirge. It is a lament concerning the princes of Israel – Ezekiel consistently calls them princes not kings, but it is not clear why. Apart from the command in verse 1, God is absent in the chapter, perhaps indicating that Israel was separated from God.

The chapter is a lament for three kings. The lioness represents Judah.[2] The two cubs may be identified as Jehoahaz, son of Josiah (who reigned briefly in 609 BC until Pharaoh Necho deposed him and took him to Egypt for lifelong imprisonment)[3] and Jehoiakim. The vine is Zedekiah. (An alternative interpretation sees the lioness as Hamutal, mother of Jehoahaz and Zedekiah and the second lion cub as Jehoiachin.) Unlike chapter 17, this chapter does not give an explanation.

This is a very negative chapter, with Ezekiel offering no hope for the future. No strong branch is left until God fulfils the promise in Isaiah to raise a Branch from the stump of Jesse[4] in the person of Jesus. Ezekiel's only message to the exiles is to lament (v 14b).

Nancy Bowen asks, 'Can communities of faith become places that nurture the capacity to lament?'[5] Laments are common in the Bible. Have modern Christians lost the aptitude to lament?

---

[1] franciscanmedia.org/franciscan-spirit-blog/biblical-laments-prayer-out-of-pain [2] Gen 49:9
[3] 2 Kings 23:31–33; Jer 22:10–12 [4] Isa 11:1 [5] N Bowen, 2010, p112

BIBLE IN A YEAR: **Job 18,19; Luke 19**

Covenant Love

'[God] will be the sure foundation for your times, a rich store of salvation and wisdom and knowledge'.[1]

Psalms 145–150 formed part of the daily morning prayer in the synagogue. Most begin 'Praise the LORD' and describe different aspects of the call to praise. Here the emphasis is on God as the one true foundation for human society, the only one who can ensure that justice prevails. Although this is a congregational hymn rather than a song of personal thanksgiving, the psalmist is far from being an observer of communal worship. He is determined to share in it personally.

Ezekiel would have appreciated the reference (v 7) to setting the prisoners (exiles) free, just as he would have enjoyed the mention of the Lord as the God of Jacob, a reminder that the beleaguered exiles were still part of God's chosen people going back to the patriarchs – Abraham, Isaac and Jacob. The warning not to put one's trust in princes and other humans (v 3) was also a major

theme of Ezekiel's message to the exiles. Instead, the exiles, along with those singing this hymn of praise, were to put their hope in the Lord (v 5). A difficult part of Ezekiel's message was to explain why the covenant-making God of Jacob was not coming to their rescue. It was because God's people had strayed from God to such an extent that when God 'frustrates the ways of the wicked' (v 9) it includes them.

The picture of the Lord that the psalmist paints is wide-ranging. God is the Creator and Sustainer, the covenant God. God frustrates the plans of the wicked, but a major emphasis in the description of God's attributes is the way he comes to the aid of the needy, identified as the oppressed, the hungry, the prisoners, the blind, the foreigners, the widows, the fatherless and those who are bowed down. God's love reaches everywhere.

How do we speak up for justice in our divided and perhaps inherently unfair society?

[1] Isa 33:6

BIBLE IN A YEAR: **Job 20,21; Luke 20**

Déjà Vu All Over Again

Faith is about trusting God even when we don't understand his plan.

14 August 591 BC. The abominations that were depicted allegorically in chapter 16 are now described historically. Ezekiel describes Israel's history in Egypt, the wilderness, the Promised Land and the Exile in terms of a recurring pattern of God's grace, Israel's rebellion, God's anger and God's protecting his name. The elders may have been hoping for an encouraging word. Instead, they are put on trial! Christopher Wright points out that Ezekiel is not writing a dispassionate history but a rhetorical parody of Israel's history with grossly distorted caricatures to make his point, probably wanting to leave his readers feeling uncomfortable.[1]

As he expounds history in the light of God's honour and the nation's disregard of him,[2] Ezekiel is echoing the Pentateuch tradition, where Moses pleaded with God based on exactly this consideration, reminding God that he had a reputation to think about (Exod 32:11–14; Num 14:13–20). Concern for God's name would resonate with Ezekiel as a priest. Nancy Bowen suggests that this is a 'difficult concept that God's motivation is his own name and that he gives Israel a second chance only to avoid being "dissed" by the other nations'.[3]

Katheryn Darr calls verses 25 and 26 'one of the Bible's most troubling texts'.[4] How could God give the people bad and defiling laws? While this is the only instance in the Bible where God 'defiles', Ezekiel is not alone in attributing disturbing actions to God![5] Ezekiel was reflecting the view that God is responsible for everything, whether causing it or allowing it. This is a difficult passage and it cannot be explained away in a sentence or two.

The biggest passion of Ezekiel's ministry is that people would know that God is the Lord. What can we do to help people to acknowledge God in our society?

[1] C Wright, 2001, p160 [2] J Stafford Wright, *Lamentations–Daniel*, SU, 1969, p 34 [3] N Bowen, 2010, p115 [4] Kathryn Darr, *Ezekiel*, Abington Press, 2001, p1290 [5] Eg 1 Kings 22:19–23; Exod 9:12; Isa 6:10,11

BIBLE IN A YEAR: **Job 22,23; Psalm 85**

His Terrible Swift Sword

'The highest place that heaven affords / is his by sovereign right.'[1]

Ezekiel is told to 'set his face' (v 2), which is often a prelude to some dramatic action. The chapter has four sections held together by the 'sword', with the word occurring 20 times in the chapter. When the sword has done its job, fire will burn up the rest – see Joshua, Judges and Isaiah for examples of the sword and fire as weapons of mass destruction. We can imagine Ezekiel speaking out his prophecy while brandishing and whirling a sword in the sunlight for dramatic effect. The sword seems like 'a veritable Excalibur with a life of its own'.[2] It is the sword of Nebuchadnezzar, but in reality it is the sword of God, executing divine judgement. Then Ezekiel acts out Nebuchadnezzar coming to a fork in the road and tossing a coin to decide whether to attack Jerusalem or the Ammonites. He did not have a coin, so he used the approved contemporary methods of divination: an oracle and examining the liver of a sacrificed animal (v 21)! It all pointed to an attack on Jerusalem. However, verses 28–32 show that the Ammonites would get their comeuppance later.

In verse 3, Ezekiel acknowledges that the casualties of war will include both the righteous and the wicked. Recent conflicts show us the indiscriminate horrors of war.

The good news comes in the second half of verse 27. Although the immediate future is bleak, with the message of coming judgement, sword and fire destroying the city, Ezekiel also foresees a day, echoing Genesis 49:10, when the crown will be restored to 'great David's greater Son'.[3] He will be exalted to the highest place with a 'name that is above every name, that at the name of Jesus every knee should bow'.[4] Amen!

What hope or encouragement does this chapter give to people who are currently living through the horrors of war?

[1] T Kelly, 1769–1855, 'The head that once' [2] Leslie C Allen, *Word Biblical Commentary, Ezekiel 20–48*, 1990, p26 [3] J Montgomery, 1771–1854 'Hail to the Lord's Anointed' [4] Phil 2:9,10

BIBLE IN A YEAR: **Job 24–26; Luke 21**

Ezekiel 22

Melting Point

Thank God for Jesus, 'the Lamb of God, who takes away the sin of the world!'[1]

The previous chapter, with its symbolism of the sword, painted a picture of destruction without mercy. Chapter 22 provides the rationale for such ruthlessness, telling the inside story of Jerusalem's fate. Ezekiel preaches a three-point sermon, with each point introduced with 'the word of the LORD came to me' (vs 1,17,23). The sins were ethical and religious, sexual, social and judicial: uncleanness, adultery, incest, bribery, exploitation and racketeering. The princes, priests, officials, prophets and the people of the land are individually and collectively guilty. It was enough to make God strike his hands together in anger (v 13). In contrast to chapter 18, there is no historical survey and there are no reasoned arguments to develop the case. Already in the second sentence of the chapter, Ezekiel is invited to pass judgement on his nation.

God's answer is to put Judah in a smelting furnace. The hearers might have assumed that the refining process would remove their impurities or that suffering would strengthen their character. Ezekiel goes in a different direction – the metals will be melted not refined; there will be no end product.[2] Allen notes that, in smelting, the silver content would often be less than 0.5 per cent, but here God pronounces that it's all slag, devoid of silver.[3]

In verse 30, God is reported as unsuccessfully looking for someone 'to stand before me in the gap'. In chapter 14, Ezekiel has referred to Noah, Job and Daniel in the past, but no such godly person can be found now. Jeremiah would have fitted the bill in terms of his faith and righteousness, but he probably did not have sufficient standing to be listened to. The chapter has no happy ending. The people will be consumed by God's anger, a just punishment for 'all they have done' (v 31).

What aspects of your character need to be refined by God's fire?[4]

[1] John 1:29 [2] N Bowen, 2010, p135 [3] LC Allen, 1990, p37 [4] Mal 3:3

BIBLE IN A YEAR: **Job 27,28; Luke 22**

Girls Behaving Badly

**'We have erred, and strayed from your ways like lost sheep ...
O Lord, have mercy upon us, miserable offenders.'[1]**

Another shocking and disturbing chapter. Commentators have had a field day in headlining it: 'Girls Gone wild', 'The best little whorehouse in Jerusalem', 'Cinderella and the ugly sisters in reverse'.[2] The language is distasteful, indelicate, graphic and vulgar, even pornographic. Ezekiel wants to get the reader's attention.

The style is similar to that of chapter 16, but this chapter involves Samaria as well as Jerusalem. Adultery here symbolises foreign alliances, not primarily idolatry. Israel and Judah are referred to by their capitals, Samaria and Jerusalem, as two harlot sisters whose names mean 'her tent and 'my tent is in her', either referring to tents of worship or of adultery.[3] The names have a matching quality, like Tweedledum and Tweedledee.[4] Ezekiel, motivated by passion for God's honour, is trying to make Judah see that everything they believe about the northern kingdom is more shockingly true about themselves.

This chapter is relevant to us today in helping us to see sin as God does. Persistent sin is not just 'something for which God gives us a bad mark'.[5] Sin is serious, resulting in disastrous consequences and separation from God. The leaders of God's people are accused of putting their trust in foreign alliances rather than in God. Is there a parallel with how we put our trust in materialism, following the patterns of our society, pursuing self-advancement rather than devotion to God? In verse 32, Ezekiel uses an image, which is common in the Old Testament, of drinking from a cup. This reminds us of Jesus, as recorded in Matthew 20:22 and 26:39, who used the image to refer to his own death – which was the only way to solve for ever the problem of human sin.

Reflect on how far short of God's standard you have fallen and thank God for the death of Jesus through which you are reconciled to God.

---

[1] The General Confession, *Book of Common Prayer*, Church of England, 1552 [2] N Bowen, 2010, p139,142; C Wright, 2001, p145 [3] 2 Sam 16:22 [4] LC Allen, 1990, p48 [5] JS Wright, 1969, p38

BIBLE IN A YEAR: **Job 29,30; Luke 23**

Death of Ezekiel's Wife

'Praise be to the God and Father of our Lord Jesus Christ, the Father of compassion and the God of all comfort, who comforts us in all our troubles'.[1]

Here is another cooking-pot analogy, although it is not clear if Ezekiel spoke in words or if he acted out the parable, potentially ruining a valuable cooking pot. Here the pot is destroyed to illustrate God's declaration that Jerusalem cannot be saved: 'I will not have pity' (v 14). These are words of terrible finality – God's patience is exhausted.

God tells Ezekiel that he is to lose his wife. This is almost another acted parable to illustrate that what Ezekiel's wife means to him, the Temple means to the people and how they will suffer its loss. It is only from this passage that we know that Ezekiel was married. His wife is not named. The chapter gives us an unusual glimpse of Ezekiel as a man devoted to his wife, who is the delight of his eyes. We cannot begin to imagine his inner anguish when he is told she is to die. All the more so as he is neither to show grief nor conduct funeral rites, but continue with his prophetic work. One may wonder whether he told her how the day would end.

Life cannot have been easy for her. If Ezekiel was only 34 she may have been only in her twenties. Initially strictly vetted against the requirements for a priest's wife,[2] she would have been honoured to have an important and respected husband, who would serve in the Temple in Jerusalem. Then the exile dashed all those hopes. In exile she finds herself living with a man who virtually starved himself to death before her eyes, who was the butt of everything from mockery to hatred and 'whose unpredictable eccentricity made her house a virtual tourist site'.[3] Wives, like prophets, who sacrifice their priorities for the sake of the kingdom will not go unrewarded.

The loss of his wife was a great personal tragedy for Ezekiel. Is there someone who has lost a loved one that you can support and pray for?

[1] 2 Cor 1:3,4 [2] Lev 21 [3] C Wright, 2001, p215

BIBLE IN A YEAR: **Job 31,32; Psalms 86,87**

A Strange Interlude

'Our Father in heaven, hallowed be your name, your kingdom come, your will be done, on earth as it is in heaven.'[1]

Ezekiel 24 ended with the news of the imminent siege of Jerusalem. Just when the reader is desperate to know what happens next, there is a commercial break! The editor inserts eight chapters of prophecies against foreign nations before resuming the news from Jerusalem in chapter 33. Bowen says that the only people likely to read these chapters are students required to write an essay on them;[2] Christopher Wright suggests that in terms of the likelihood of finding spiritual food and comfort for your soul, these chapters rank alongside the genealogies in Chronicles and the regulations on mildew in Leviticus![3]

Here we have oracles against four neighbouring nations, with a repeated formula 'This is what the Sovereign LORD says ... because ... therefore'. It was characteristic for prophets to survey other nations of the world to demonstrate the Lord's sovereignty over them as well as over Israel. The purpose is to show that God is God of the whole earth, with something to say about the history and destiny of nations. Further, as the audience for these oracles is not the nations but the exilic community, it was encouraging for Judah to know that God would judge the nations.[4] A common accusation against the nations is that they gloated over Judah's plight (vs 3,8,15) and didn't gave a hand. To be fair, it is hard to 'lend a helping hand when busy using it for gleeful clapping'.[5]

This is Ezekiel's theological response to the nations who threatened Judah or challenged God's dominion – particularly Moab, which is accused of denying Israel's unique relationship with God. Ezekiel is rejecting the contemporary view that Judah's God would not be able to protect them against the Babylonian god, Marduk, any more than the gods of the nations.

A concern that God's name should be honoured is central to Ezekiel's prophecies: how do we prioritise God's name in our society?

[1] Matt 6:9,10 [2] N Bowen, 2010, p151 [3] C Wright, 2001, p233 [4] JB Taylor, 1969, p184,185
[5] N Bowen, 2010, p154

BIBLE IN A YEAR: **Job 33,34; Luke 24**

Psalm 147

Home at Last

'Ransomed, healed, restored, forgiven, / who like me his praise should sing?'[1]

This post-exilic psalm sees the return from Babylonian exile and the restoration of Jerusalem as a reason to offer praise and worship to God, acknowledging God's power and his gracious care of the covenant people, whose unique status is acknowledged (v 20). The heartbreak of exile has been replaced by the healing comfort of being home again. The security and well-being of the post-exilic community were seen as divine gifts.

The argument goes from the particular, through the general to the universal:[2] God provides for Israel specifically, cares for the broken-hearted generally and controls the heavens. It is the same Creator God who flung the stars into space who set the captives free from Babylonia. That God's power avails at every level should enable us to trust him with our particular problem, be it great or small. The tragedy is that humans are so prone to seek their sufficiency in money, possessions, materialism, etc.

The references to God sending out his word (vs 15–19) are striking. It is the word of God which shapes nature and history. The world is not left to its own devices, but God controls it through his Word. In Isaiah, God reminds us that his Word 'will not return to me empty, but will accomplish what I desire and achieve the purpose for which I sent it'[3] and in Hebrews that it is 'alive and active. Sharper than any double-edged sword, it penetrates even to dividing soul and spirit'.[4] As Christians, we have the deeper meaning of Jesus, identified as the Word of God incarnate.

Ezekiel and the psalmist often saw God's hand in events: what evidence of God's hand do you see in contemporary events?

[1] Henry F Lyte, 1793–1847, 'Praise, my soul, the King of heaven' [2] HL Ellison, 1967, p122 [3] Isa 55:11 [4] Heb 4:12

BIBLE IN A YEAR: **Job 35,36; Philippians 1**

The Day of the Lord

'... at the name of Jesus every knee should bow, in heaven and on earth and under the earth, and every tongue acknowledge that Jesus Christ is Lord'.[1]

Like Jeremiah, Ezekiel had the difficult task of communicating to his Judaean hearers an unpatriotic message, the prophetic truth that God's judgement was at work in the fall of Jerusalem. Ezekiel had to work hard to dispel the commonly held, but vain, hope that salvation would come for the people of Judah through the assistance of Egypt, emphasising that the Judaeans 'had put their political and providential eggs into the wrong basket'.[2] He had previously attempted to show the exiles that God's judgement on Jerusalem was as justified as it was certain. In fact, Egypt was now facing the same destiny as Israel itself: namely, the day of the Lord.[3]

The breaking of Pharaoh's arm (v 21) may refer to the defeat of his army, which attempted to relieve the siege of Jerusalem.[4] The Babylonian attack on Egypt could be the breaking of his other arm. There is a certain irony that one of Pharaoh Hophra's titles was 'mighty of arm'. Big Chief Strong Arm had become Little Chief Broken Arm.[5]

The day of the Lord is a familiar Old Testament concept.[6] It was originally a term that summarised Israel's expectations that God would defeat their enemies and raise Israel itself up in victory and salvation, but for Ezekiel it meant the day of God's judgement. The final day is yet to come when God will put an end to all sin everywhere. Interim days of the Lord become patterns for and previews of the final day. Having previously mentioned it in chapter 7 in relation to Israel, Ezekiel now proclaims it as a day of judgement for Egypt. The end of the story is summed up in the familiar refrain: 'Then they will know that I am the LORD' (v 26).

In our eagerness to communicate to people the love of God, how can we proclaim God's judgement without appearing judgemental?

[1] Phil 2:10,11 [2] LC Allen, 1990, p117 [3] C Wright, 2001, p250 [4] Jer 37:5 [5] C Wright, 2001, p251 [6] Isa 2:12–21; Joel 1:15; 2:2,3; Amos 5:18–20; Zeph 1:7,14–18

BIBLE IN A YEAR: **Job 37,38; Psalm 88**

John 7–11

SEE AND KNOW

In these next weeks, we will be accompanying Jesus closely. John's purpose is that we should see who Jesus is and have life in his name. John loves the word 'know': the whole-bodied sort of 'know', involving head and heart and will. Whether you have travelled with Jesus for a lifetime or are taking your first tentative steps or are still making up your mind, this is dynamite. Tread slowly.

We walk with a varied cast of companions: Jesus' brothers, pilgrims, onlookers, religious leaders, a shamed woman, a blind man and his parents, Lazarus, Martha and Mary. John lets us eavesdrop on heated arguments, as confrontations regarding Jesus' identity and credentials escalate. We hear murmurings of puzzled crowds seeking to make sense of Jesus' astonishing claims: 'I am the light of the world', 'Come to me and drink', 'Before Abraham was born, I am', 'I am the good shepherd', 'My father and I are one', 'I am the resurrection and the life'. We have ringside seats as Jesus draws close to the overlooked and the heartbroken. We witness unfolding movements in misunderstanding and mistrust, blindness and belief.

We are given vivid eyewitness details of times and places. The feasts of Tabernacles and Dedication in Jerusalem largely frame the interactions. These festivals remind participants of their continuing history as the people of God. The opposition, which dominates much of the narrative, grows because he declares that he has come to fulfil these celebrations and institutions. He is the long-awaited Messiah. The establishment stakeholders are shocked and outraged. We feel an ugly atmosphere of foreboding, as repeatedly arrest and stoning are threatened. Poignantly, we also see Jesus responding in love and obedience to the Father and his timetable, his 'hour'. Amid troubling times and competing claims, then and now, we are invited to draw close to Jesus. Come with him, as he reveals his heart and purpose.

Fiona Barnard

Platforms and Sidelines

'My times are in your hands':[1] pause, entrusting this moment, this day, to God.

'Seize the day! Secure a platform. You are doing great tricks. Everyone loves your stories. But not here. This is the back of beyond. Why not grab the stage at a big festival? If you have something life-changing to offer, shouldn't you be at the heart of a religious zone, where the movers and shakers, the educated and influencers, gather?'

Picture Jesus walking, his brothers' proposals buzzing like flies in his ears. He shakes them off, hurt perhaps by their daredevil teasing, their delusion concerning everything about him, even after all these years together. They have gone with a pilgrim crowd to the feast of Tabernacles. Jesus has delayed his journey until the festival is half over. En route, he's passed rural homes and, now, city dwellings hugged by temporary shelters covered with branches. He's watched families inside, their tables groaning with recently harvested grapes and olives, recalling God's care for his people, from ancient wilderness wanderings until today. The flimsy tents contrast with the grandeur of the Temple coming into view. This place, the focus of the feast, scarcely reflects the sense of fragility and dependence on God which is its theological core. On this stage, its leaders hog the limelight, basking in political power, controlling the religious system and voices through fear. They choose to ignore the prophets' vital role as God's mouthpieces from the sidelines.

What is in Jesus' heart as he arrives in Jerusalem? Surrounded by this ancient feast of gratitude and grace, he is beset by murderous hatred, cynical murmuring, familial misunderstanding, feverish curiosity. Yet he is also absorbed in loving obedience to the Father. Passover in six months, not Tabernacles, will be the right time for a very different type of revelation.

How does your church advertise the truth of Jesus? When image and PR are so integral to modern communication, how can you stay close to his ways?

[1] Ps 31:15

BIBLE IN A YEAR: **Job 39,40; Philippians 2**

John 7:14–24

Tunnels, Tramlines or Trust?

'You, God, are my God, earnestly I seek you ... I have seen you in the sanctuary and beheld your power and your glory.'[1] Pause to seek, to behold.

John is the original vox pop reporter, albeit without a camera! As we weave our way through this chapter, and indeed most chapters, he invites us to see and hear what is happening around Jesus. Sense the movement and buzz as the crowds in Jerusalem, pilgrims and locals, voice their questions and opinions about Jesus. Let the snippets of conversation and debate, in the streets and Temple courts, resonate with you. As the lens picks out talking heads, I wonder if you recognise the confusion, censure, fear, faith, envy, outrage and wistfulness reflected in those you know.

Some marvel at the wisdom of Jesus' extraordinary teaching. Others are scandalised by it and by the audacity of his behaviour. Jesus' CV includes no formal rabbinic learning. He does not cite other religious teachers. Who taught him? What are his credentials? Engaging with the general melee, Jesus takes time with the questioners: 'The one who sent me is my authority. I speak his truth. I aim to honour him, not to put myself forward.' To those claiming faithfulness to the law, he dares to suggest that tunnel vision has caused them to miss its crucial life-giving purpose. He gives an example. They override their strict application of 'no work on the Sabbath' so that boys can be circumcised on the eighth day. However, when Jesus brings physical, social and spiritual wholeness to a disabled man on the Sabbath, they are fixated on his breaking the law by carrying his mat.[2]

How are views, then and now, so divided over Jesus? Jesus suggests that the answer lies in a heart attitude, which trumps any clever argument (v 17). Those genuinely open to God eventually grasp the truth about Jesus. Have you not marvelled at seekers believing 'in order to understand'?[3]

As you meet individuals wrestling with questions, doubts or objections, how might you model a faith that is focused on Jesus, rather than bound by tramline beliefs and practices?

---

[1] Ps 63:1,2 [2] John 5:9,10 [3] Augustine of Hippo, 354–430

BIBLE IN A YEAR: **Job 41,42; Philippians 3**

Coming and Going

'We have seen his glory, the glory of the one and only Son, who came from the Father, full of grace and truth.'[1] Ponder this marvel.

'Last weekend, I watched a film about Jesus. I didn't know his story, but I loved him!' The international learners in my English class always teach me to see life and faith from unexpected angles. Over many years, I have pondered different responses to the person of Jesus. For this Chinese woman, Jesus' kindness and healing powers were hugely attractive. Initially open to reading the Bible, her admiration did not lead to worship. An Eastern European told me how faith was important to her – until she concluded that her church was self-serving and she lost interest in Jesus. Another time, following an Easter play, a Muslim whispered, 'I believe Jesus will return one day. Do you?'

As I overhear discussions in today's passage, the faces of my students merge with the pilgrims, Jerusalemites and religious leaders. For each, the crucial question is, 'Who exactly is Jesus?' Is he an anti-establishment nuisance? A threat? A miracle worker? The long-awaited Messiah? A blasphemer? A madman? What fascinates me is that, disregarding all good apologetics, Jesus does not argue the points, but presents the curious and the critical with a deeper challenge. It concerns his origin and mission. It focuses on where he has come from and where he is going. Amid speculation in a chattering city, he cries out, 'I am from him and he sent me … I am with you for only a short time, and then I am going to the one who sent me' (vs 29,33).

Any conclusion about Jesus, any commitment to him, takes us beyond the man in first-century Jerusalem to his unique divine origin and purpose from all eternity. Genuine faith disregards human bias and distortion. It grasps Jesus' uncompromising claim to know God completely and to speak his truth.

What will bring your contacts to a full, life-giving knowledge of Jesus? Pray that the Spirit will dissolve misunderstanding, apathy and distraction.

[1] John 1:14

BIBLE IN A YEAR: **Mark 1; Philippians 4**

John 7:37–52

Touch, See, Taste, Hear

'With joy you will draw water from the wells of salvation.'[1] Bring your thirst to Jesus now. Fill your cup with his ever-flowing goodness and drink slowly.

How do observers become participants in the faith? Any bystanders had little choice but to be caught up in the stunning spectacle in Jerusalem during the feast of Tabernacles. Surrounded by temporary booths dotted all over the city, they would be engulfed in the daily processions as people waved branches and citrus fruit in gratitude for God's provision of harvest. They would hear singing of psalms as they followed the crowd: 'Give thanks to the LORD'.[2] When water was carried from the pool of Siloam and poured down the Temple steps, they would witness the enactment of God's provision for their ancestors in the wilderness and the blessing of rain for themselves. Perhaps they would feel splashes on their feet in this scene, reminiscent of Ezekiel's ancient vision of a torrent emerging from God's Temple to flood a dry world.[3] They would catch the scent of longing for the Messianic age expressed so fully in body, mind and spirit through the festival's sights and sounds, lights and rituals. Full immersion.

In this feast, however, there is abundantly more for those who have a heart to hear and see. Jesus' cry pierces the joyful hullabaloo, claiming to be the one to which it all points: 'Let anyone who is thirsty, come to me' (v 37). He is the focus, their deepest desire, the answer to their prayers.

It is ironic that such devotion does not recognise immediately the one for whom it seeks: the protagonist and the director of the drama. Often it is the religious participants who have more barriers to faith than the onlookers. In the spiritual journey, the openness of Nicodemus (v 50) is significant: willingness to explore, to examine, to encounter. I wonder what he made of his experience that climactic day?

Picture observers you know. How might a more sensory expression of faith facilitate their becoming part of the community and the story of Jesus? How might it distract?

[1] Isa 12:3 [2] Eg Ps 136:1 [3] Ezek 47:1–12

BIBLE IN A YEAR: **Mark 2; Psalm 89**

God Bows before Sinners

'Search me, God, and know my heart; test me and know my anxious thoughts. See if there is any offensive way in me, and lead me in the way everlasting'.[1]

Tell me, ancient scribe Reuben: what do you remember most about that day? When you dragged (only) the woman from her adulterous bed to the busy Temple court. Was it the noise? Her cries of protest dimming to a whimper amid the hustle of city life. The Galilean accent of Jesus telling a story, the laughs and exclamations of the listening crowd. The lull when you interrupted him, depositing there your human visual aid, your case study. The hush which felt endless and deafening as your test question hung in the air unanswered. The piercing invitation Jesus gave to the sinless to set the stoning in motion. The eventual shuffling of feet as each accuser dispersed.

Reuben, what do you recall most vividly about that scene? Was it the body movements which took on a wordless eloquence? Jesus sitting with the ease of a teacher, surrounded by the curious in rapt attention. His stooping form, responding to your confrontation by turning his face away from everyone, to doodle in the sand at his feet. The way he straightened himself up to look into the eyes of each one, including you, as he finally responded with his own challenge. His bending down again, to write in the dust, offering space for you to stop and think. I wonder: did that mesmerising finger look anything like the finger scribing God's commandments at Mount Sinai, the law you claimed to love?

All these years later, Reuben, what lingers in your heart? As you walked away, did some of the shame you poured on the woman stick to you? As you visualise her standing there, exposed, condemned, alone, did her public disgrace reveal something hidden in you? As you left Jesus with her that day, what did you want him to say to her? What do you wish he might say to you now?

Where are you in this story? Imagine you are there and watch for what Jesus might be saying to you.

---

[1] Ps 139:23,24

BIBLE IN A YEAR: **Mark 3; Colossians 1**

Psalm 148

Giddy Glory

'Come near to God and he will come near to you.'[1] Imagine yourself walking into God's presence, then kneeling before him in quiet expectation. Breathe deeply and wait.

Flying in a plane gives you a different perspective on things. High in the open air, you look down on mountain ranges, vast forests, a plethora of vegetation, deserts, seas, white clouds, a hazy infinitude. As night falls, the extravagance called sunset performs the Maker's final fling, effortlessly casting ever-changing yellows, reds and oranges across the horizon, soon replaced by darkness, moon and stars. Descending, you may survey palaces, slums teeming with tiny shacks, ancient ruins and glistening skyscrapers, busy streets and empty plots, displaying a range of human experience, all within a few airborne minutes. Around you on the aeroplane, strong and frail, male and female, old and young, showcase a life cycle of mutual dependence. Your eyes feast on what the psalmist could only imagine. Magnificence is everywhere. Yet God is more magnificent.

Staggering, beautiful, diverse, grand: how can you begin to describe even a slice of life on this planet God has made? With a word, he brought it all into existence and continues to sustain it with the utmost care and attention. Physical terrains and living beings in all their colour and character, beauty and bounty, delight and diversity exhibit the Lord's greatness. In their very being, all wriggling, flying, jumping, swimming, breathing creatures celebrate their divine craftsman. Wonder is everywhere. Yet God is more wonderful.

Today, whether your vision is clouded or clear, lift your eyes to your Maker, whose name is higher than the furthest galaxy. Poignantly, he invites you to come close to his tender heart. Join the awe-filled symphony of worship which is both immense and intimate. Glory is everywhere. Yet God is more glorious.

Spend time today simply enjoying God's world, whether through art or photography, a view from your window or in your imagination.

[1] James 4:8

BIBLE IN A YEAR: **Mark 4; Colossians 2**

Can't See, Won't See

'... with you is the fountain of life; in your light we see light.'[1] Take time to consider what this means to you as you come to the Light.

'Don't look at the sun. It will blind you.' There were warnings galore when a rare eclipse caused great fascination across the UK. Eye masks with pin pricks were recommended to protect fragile eyes from the glory. As Jesus cries out, 'I am the light' (v 12), amid the daily lighting of lamps at the feast of Tabernacles, I wonder if part of the fracas which ensues is because truly no one can look at God and live.

What a striking setting for Jesus to announce his identity and his invitation! For seven days, the golden candelabras have thrown light on the busy Temple courtyard where worshippers bring their offerings. Joyous dancing with fiery torches has filled the nights. In an age without street lighting, the glow of celebration has lit up the city spectacularly. Then Jesus' voice calls out in the blaze, 'I am the light of the world'.

As the festival lights recall the pillar of fire, the guiding presence of God in the wilderness wanderings, Jesus is saying, 'I am that presence among you now: God's presence. Come after me on life's journey. I will guide you always'. Furthermore, his reach is not restricted to the Jewish Temple courts: he is the Light of the world. Astonishingly, when pilgrims are about to scatter home, he claims for himself God's ancient promise to the anointed Servant and Messiah: 'I will also make you a light for the Gentiles, that my salvation may reach to the ends of the earth.'[2]

No one can argue light into existence: it simply is there. He is there. Ironically, the religious leaders don't recognise in Jesus and his work the God they claim to know. So fixated are they on religious legalism and control, that they have closed their eyes tight to God's life-giving Light.

Is there a subtle danger that leaders holding religious torches might point them like searchlights at others, lest the shadows of their own hearts be shamefully exposed?

[1] Ps 36:9 [2] Isa 49:6

BIBLE IN A YEAR: **Mark 5; Psalm 90**

John 8:21–30

Seeing the Unseeable

'... God ... made his light shine in our hearts to give us the light of the knowledge of God's glory displayed in the face of Christ.'[1] What do you see?

'What is your image of God?' I find that agnostics and religious believers alike can be reluctant to describe their perceptions, whether through ignorance, laziness, indifference or fear of offence. Some attempt a feeble stab at it which makes God sound like a vague idea or force. Others talk about someone 'being there', a comfortable, yet faceless presence. Internationals in my English classes engage variously with often very definite cultural beliefs concerning what God demands. Eloquent atheists can be more forthcoming when I ask, 'Tell me about the God in whom you don't believe'. Privately, Christians struggling with prayer may uncover a divine caricature, a barrier to intimacy. Even the faithful are tempted to make God in their own image, saying, 'My God wouldn't be like this...'

Yet this ambiguity is not new. How can those 'from below' understand a God 'from above'? No wonder Jesus' interlocutors are puzzled. Their God is very different from the one this flesh and blood Jesus claims to represent and reveal. His 'I am ...' statements have a blasphemous whiff of divine pretension. To many, he speaks in riddles, contrasting coming and going, being of this world or another, of dying in sin or pleasing the Father. Yet Jesus pinpoints the obstacle not as bewilderment, but as deadly unbelief. Ironically, the one sent to show them the Father is rejected.

In our prayers, we too are not 'left ... alone' (v 29). The Father has poured all of himself into Jesus. He is the image of the invisible God, a person with a face. He speaks our language. He need not be a stranger. Revelation is on his terms, not ours. Startlingly, on a shameful cross, he is highly honoured, bridging heaven and earth in his broken body.

Poignantly, amid the controversy and mystery, many believe in Jesus. Pray by name for individuals who struggle to respond to Jesus.

[1] 2 Cor 4:6

BIBLE IN A YEAR: **Mark 6; Colossians 3**

Family Likeness

'Guide me in your truth and teach me, for you are God my Saviour, and my hope is in you all day long.'[1]

I vividly remember an encounter as a schoolgirl with a couple who had been imprisoned following the Iranian revolution. They brought posters with black words such as 'hatred', 'envy', 'selfishness', 'pride' and 'greed' like bricks one on top of the other. 'These are what really binds us', they said, 'not locks and keys'. In the centre was the shape of a person through whom a sun-bathed scene of vibrant green fields and mountains beckoned. Below were the words, 'If the Son sets you free, you will be free indeed'.

As the mob around Jesus becomes angrier, the gloves are off. When accusations are fired at him, now with words, soon with nails, Jesus responds bluntly. His truth penetrates sin-soaked layers of deceit in devilish family likeness: stubborn presuppositions, idolatrous 'orthodoxy', wilful deafness, addiction to power. In the struggle to determine truth, source is key.

Jesus maintains that truth and, through it, freedom are not found in blessed genes and ancestry. They cannot be secured through sheer birthright and religious adherence. Truth comes through him. Genuine disciples not only assent to his words, but walk in the light of his teaching, recognising that it comes from the Father.

I wonder: what is in Jesus' heart as he speaks these piercing words? How is his tone of voice? When we take the high ground in theological arguments, imagining we are defending the gospel, we easily become as self-righteous and twitchy as Jesus' opponents. The chisel of truth Jesus applies to their wall of empty legitimacy is held by a hand which will soon be crushed for their iniquities. In the harshest of public exchanges is the merciful invitation to step into the freedom of living the Father's way through him alone. He is the truth.

What does Jesus' gift of freedom look like in my life? How could it transform my community?

---

[1] Ps 25:5

BIBLE IN A YEAR: **Mark 7; Colossians 4**

John 8:48–59

What *Did* Abraham See?

"'I am the Alpha and the Omega," says the Lord God, "who is, and who was, and who is to come, the Almighty."'[1] Lift your heart to him.

What *did* you see, Abraham (v 56)? When God called you to a radically new life of obedience and trust... when you and Sarah were childless, old and barren... when he promised to bless the peoples of the earth through your offspring... what filled your faithful mind's eye? When you contemplated the myriad stars in the dark night sky, did you picture the faces of your descendants shining with God's light? When your toes felt the heat of millions of grains of sand, could you imagine them in their own land, blessing the world? When at long last you gazed into your baby son's eyes, the incarnation of God's everlasting covenant with you, what was that joy like? Did you, as the rabbis maintained, have a vision of the coming Messiah amid your laughter?

Abraham, as you scrutinised the distant horizons of time, how did you envisage your descendants enjoying the fruits of the promise? Claiming physical and spiritual kinship with you, yet no longer knowing your God? Religiously unwilling to imitate your obedience to God's radical call to a new life? Did God whisper in your ear, 'I will go to introduce myself to your offspring. I will fulfil our covenant perfectly'? Could you have conceived that your God would be unrecognised, deemed a liar, a heretic, a crazy man, demon-possessed?

Abraham, when you assured Isaac, 'God himself will provide the lamb for the burnt offering, my son',[2] could you have imagined you were mouthing echoes of another Father, another Son? In the supreme irony of your children's murderous intent, Temple stones in their hands, could your joy stretch to see the Messiah's coming glory? In that space, held only by faith and not reason, what was it like to be overjoyed? To visualise the blinding splendour of Jesus' day?

Eternal God, you keep your promises. Help me to honour you today and to trust you with all I don't see or understand.

[1] Rev 1:8 [2] Gen 22:8

BIBLE IN A YEAR: **Mark 8; 1 Thessalonians 1**

Vision

'The Lord is my light and my salvation'.[1]

I will never forget the collective gasp as Jesus cured a blind beggar. We were watching a film about Jesus with some non-Christian friends. They had never seen anything like it and were amazed. What a delight to witness! Yet it was also a rebuke, because I was so used to Jesus giving sight to the blind, my sense of wonder had frayed. In this account of Jesus giving a man his vision, we also watch an acted parable with a lively cast of characters. We get behind-the-scenes insight into God's glorious kingdom work, full of drama, humour and warning: the Light of God shines into physical and spiritual darkness, highlighting truth and sham, bringing judgement and restoration.

At the heart of the story is a beggar, blind from birth. He cannot contribute to family finances or feel the satisfaction of a day's work. As a disabled man, he cannot participate in Temple worship. Casual passers-by engage in theological debate: 'Whose sin is responsible for his pitiful state?' Sadly, he is not the first nor the last person to receive blame on top of misery. Yet Jesus sees him and speaks to him, touching his useless eyes with mud. He gives him something purposeful to do: 'Go ... wash in the Pool of Siloam' (v 7).

Why Siloam? Fresh suggestions came with the discovery in 2004 of an Olympic-sized pool at the actual Siloam, much larger than the one previously visited by tourists. This was a vast place of cleansing, where weary pilgrims arriving in Jerusalem prepared to set foot in the Temple. From Siloam, they ascended the steps to where God met his holy people. As this excluded man opens his eyes, the first thing he sees is the stairway bidding him join the worshippers.[2] A journey of sight and insight beckons.

Jesus saw the blind man (v 1): Lord, today help me to notice, to really see, people with your eyes of compassion!

---

[1] Ps 27:1 [2] Andrew D Mayes, *Sensing the divine: John's word made flesh*, BRF, 2019

BIBLE IN A YEAR: **Mark 9; Psalm 91**

John 9:13–23

Blinding Light

'... the LORD gives sight to the blind, the LORD lifts up those who are bowed down'.[1] Praise him for his kindness to you.

We know the drill by now: when there is healing on the Sabbath, there is a vocal group who disapprove. In their role as religious compliance enforcers, the Pharisees interrogate various people to gather evidence against Jesus. Significantly, examining the same situation, they are at odds. Some are absorbed by the miracle and concede that it can only be done by a godly person. Strangely, they go quiet from now on. Others are fixated on a technical breach of the Sabbath law. They ignore the Old Testament consensus that a prophet is validated by the signs he performs. They interrogate the healed man about the facts and later, surprisingly, about his opinion. There is a sense of mayhem as they thrash around for alternative explanations and resort to accusations.

The light of truth can blind or give sight. While the seeing man engages with what has happened to him and, importantly, who has touched his life, his parents are intimidated by the threats and interrogation. They show little solidarity with their son. Any pleasure they had is consumed by fear and foreboding. The religious adversaries are bullies, closing their eyes to any possibility that God might actually be answering their oft-repeated prayers for salvation, thereby consigning themselves to darkness.

It is natural to distance ourselves from the villains in this story. We feel exasperated that they could be so prejudiced, so self-serving, so blind. Yet spiritual leadership can command great power. Sadly, determination to protect the faith against upstarts without the necessary credentials can lead to subtle or less-than-subtle abuses of clout and control. Defensiveness against criticism or challenge may blind us to God's very presence.

Can you think of recent instances of the light of God's truth blinding or giving sight? What happened?

[1] Ps 146:8

BIBLE IN A YEAR: **Mark 10; 1 Thessalonians 2**

Delight and Honour

'... you are a chosen people ... God's special possession, that you may declare the praises of him who called you out of darkness into his wonderful light.'[1]

'Can you speak to God in the shower?', I once asked a lovely Buddhist couple as we chatted about what prayer might mean. They looked a bit startled and replied that, for them, it had to be in the temple. So I am struck by this intriguing verse 5: 'Let his faithful people ... sing for joy on their beds'! The exuberant psalmist invites us to praise God at all times and in all places. Even the bed-bound, the insomniacs and the weary can join the worship of his privileged people. But why?

Possibly composed in the wake of a military victory or following the exile, this song celebrates the astonishing choice of the Lord. He has selected Israel, a seemingly insignificant people on the world stage, to be his own. This God, then and now, honours the humble, favours the faithful. He takes pleasure in those whom no one notices much. For the weak and overlooked, for those living in shame, this public delight in them is life-changing. As I write, I recall radiant believers dancing and singing with all their hearts over drunken shouts in a smelly South American slum: 'We are so happy, because Jesus is here. We feel love. We feel communion'. God's chosen people can sing with hope, especially those afflicted by wicked tyrants and systemic injustice. God cares. He fights for them. Their tormentors, who seem invincible, will be put to shame. Evil will not go unpunished. God's very honour is at stake.

Wherever you are today and however you feel, take time to read this psalm slowly. Let its call come to you. Choose a phrase: 'be glad', 'make music', 'a new song', 'rejoice in this honour'. Savour it. Relish his delight in you. Your Maker. Your King.

'God deliberately chose men and women that the culture overlooks and exploits and abuses, chose these "nobodies" to expose the hollow pretensions of the "somebodies"'.[2] Hallelujah!

[1] 1 Peter 2:9 [2] 1 Cor 1:27, *The Message*

BIBLE IN A YEAR: **Mark 11; 1 Thessalonians 3**

John 9:24–34

Shining

'One thing I do know. I was blind but now I see!' (v 25). Praise God for the wonder of this in your own life.

'I am full of joy and happiness to be finally able to see and identify myself confidently as a Christian', said the email. 'It is unimaginable that I would feel this a year or two ago.' Indeed it is: I had long since abandoned hope that the spiritual eyes of this Japanese researcher would ever be opened. Is there anything more exhilarating than witnessing the Spirit's miraculous intervention in a life?

Speaking of which, isn't this now-sighted man a tonic? In contrast to his apprehensive parents, he speaks his mind. In fact, it feels as though he is so thrilled by what Jesus has done for him that he is quite unhinged. Amid the toxic debate with the religious leaders, he bounces around, repeating the facts they demand, poking at their balloon-like pomposity and exposing their closed minds. They respond with insults, refusing to believe him and iterating their devotion to Moses' law. The unschooled man, excluded for a lifetime from Temple worship, teaches them a biblical lesson about whose prayers God answers. He recognises that he does not have all the answers – but he knows that he can see: the light has dawned in his darkened world. He stands as a radiant model of a life transformed. Even his neighbours struggle to recognise him.

My friend's email continues, 'My mum asked me to pray together with her since she does not know how to do it in a Christian way: I am a beginner too, but hope I am doing it correctly as I believe God has responded to me positively so far. I have been currently sharing a daily text message on "Reading the Bible every day" with both my mum and dad, which is so blissful to me. It seems contagious.' Hallelujah! New believers are the best witnesses. Their stories are indeed delightful in our eyes.

When did you last hear the testimony of a new Christian? Recall it and enjoy God's miraculous work of transformation.

BIBLE IN A YEAR: **Mark 12; Psalms 92,93**

Dawning

'My ears had heard of you but now my eyes have seen you.'[1] Lord, show me more of your lovely face!

At Easter, we witnessed the baptism of a Brazilian student who nervously set foot in church just weeks earlier. Raised by a fiercely atheist father, he described his agonised search, 'I had a hunger inside me for meaning and for what is Good, which I now realise I could only attain through faith. I felt some sense of shame in being drawn to Christ because I saw mockery of faith when I was young. But today I want to earnestly, publicly declare, without any ounce of shame or hesitation that Jesus Christ is Lord, and I totally submit myself to him.'

The light has been dawning, too, for the healed man. From simply knowing Jesus' name, to supposing he is a prophet, to insisting he must be from God, the identity of Christ is taking shape in his mind. Ironically, the dark opposition and loneliness of his position have sharpened and clarified his understanding. However, although he has heard Jesus' voice, he has never set eyes on him. Now, fresh from being harangued by the religious authorities and his expulsion from the synagogue, he meets Jesus, who has come to find him.

After the hubbub of debate and insult, a hush descends. The scene is empty but for Jesus approaching the man. Can you glimpse Jesus' delight as he searches out the heart that is ripe for the next step of faith? This is the climax: a beautiful, intensely moving personal encounter. The once blind man gazes into the eyes of the one he could only imagine before: at last, he sees the one who saw him and gifted him with vision. He meets the one who gave him everything and for whom now he has lost so much. He hears him. He sees him. He worships him. Light of the world.

This same Jesus seeks those for whom you pray, longing to grant sight and calling for grateful surrender. May his face shine on them, on you.

---

[1] Job 42:5

BIBLE IN A YEAR: **Mark 13; 1 Thessalonians 4**

John 10:1–10

Calling

'He tends his flock like a shepherd: he gathers the lambs in his arms and carries them close to his heart'.[1] **How is the Lord carrying you?**

Of all the images of Jesus, the Good Shepherd must be the favourite down through the centuries. It is ironic that in this modern world, where farming is consigned to fewer people, that it is this metaphor of Jesus that is still one of the most recognised, persistent and prevalent.

'Why are you telling us this?' the Pharisees must wonder. In the towns and villages where most inhabitants own sheep for wool, everyone knows that the hired gatekeeper, who guards the communal sheepfold overnight, is the one with the key. Of course, anyone sneaking in another way is up to no good. Countless times they have watched young shepherds coming to the pen in the morning, calling out their own flock from all the others. They have laughed at the amazing knack of silly sheep to identify their shepherd's voice and follow, because they trust he will take them to grass and water. Furthermore, the practice of shepherds staying out overnight in temporary shelters is nothing new: sometimes they have to go far in the wilderness in search of green pasture. It makes perfect sense for them to lie at the entrance like a door to protect their flocks from constant danger. 'So, Jesus, tell us something novel', his listeners might want to say.

The Pharisees don't hear his voice. They have just expelled the once blind man because his miraculous experience of salvation and freedom threatens their comfort. They won't accept that they might be the under-shepherds who have failed to defend and nourish God's people through greed and self-interest. They can't recognise Jesus as the rightful Shepherd, the fulfilment of God's age-old promises. They can make no sense of him as the Gate, open so that the sheep who hear and follow may revel in his abundant life.

I may know the truths of Jesus as shepherd, but how carefully do I listen to his voice?

[1] Isa 40:11

BIBLE IN A YEAR: **Mark 14; 1 Thessalonians 5**

En-folded

'... he is our God and we are the people of his pasture, the flock under his care.'[1] Thank the Good Shepherd that you are in his fold today.

'How is your church going?' asked a friend yesterday. Depending on my mood and recent events, I observe different things. I visualise the people who are not there, because they are distracted or have lost their faith, because they are wounded or disappointed or bitter. I watch those damaged by family or circumstance or church, both struggling and responding to the healing touch of Jesus. In worship, I marvel at God's Spirit transforming lives, through groups and conversations, amid all our fallibilities. It is amazing to witness.

This image of Jesus enlarges my vision for church, charging it with fresh expectation. Because he is the *Good* Shepherd: the noble, faithful, worthy Shepherd. No less than five times here, he describes himself as laying down his life. From their lambing, he actively watches over his sheep. He is alert to the ravaging wolves and robbers outside the fold. He recognises the threats from inside, when under-shepherds prize pay above protection. By contrast, Jesus gives up his time, strength, energy and sleep for their safety. He reveals intimate knowledge of each sheep and, in the face of danger, he faces the fate that would otherwise be theirs. As death threats against him grow, Jesus is utterly in control. He will give his life: it will not be stolen from him. Inextricably tied to laying down his life is his resurrection, when he takes it up again.

This is *our* winsome Shepherd. We are included in his heart's reach. We too are gathered into his sacrificial life and death, into intimacy with the Father. As I stand with the sinful and the sorrowful, the gifted and the grumpy, to receive the body and blood of Christ in communion, I recognise my place and purpose in the Shepherd's plan for the scattered and lost. I am filled with wonder and hope.

How is your church? What do you observe? What, by faith, do you grasp of the Shepherd's purpose for those outside the fold?

[1] Ps 95:7

BIBLE IN A YEAR: **Mark 15; 2 Thessalonians 1**

John 10:22–42

Open Eyes, Open Ears

'... you shepherds, hear the word of the LORD'.[1] Speak Lord, I am listening.

'Yes or no?' asks the interviewer; 'It is a simple question.' In our age of soundbites, demands that messages be distilled into a couple of sentences make a victim of the truth. We can be too heavy-handed, determined to squeeze people into boxes so we can shut them off if we disagree. Perhaps it always has been so: 'If you are the Messiah, tell us plainly', insist the people (v 24).

Is it significant that this exchange occurs at the Festival of Dedication (v 22), when Jews recall the 164 BC purification of the Temple after it had been appallingly desecrated? Jesus' questioners are reliving the military and political victory which recovered Jerusalem from the Seleucid Empire. As they light each festal candle, they are celebrating freedom to worship in their rededicated Temple. This triumph was hard-fought and defended fiercely. The tragic irony is that they fail to recognise Jesus as the dazzling fulfilment of the feast. Over the months, they have labelled him mad and demon-possessed, now a blasphemer.

Jesus will not answer 'yes or no', because their assumptions are blinkered and their messianic expectations are rigid. If only they could hear what he is really saying! He describes the unity of will and work which he shares with the Father. He reminds them of the scriptural precedent of those set apart to be called 'gods' and 'sons of the Most High' (v 34).[2] He points to his life-giving miracles. He is the true Temple, enabling God's people to worship him. So, in rejecting him, they become the desecrated. Jesus leaves and returns to the Jordan where it all began, where John declared the coming of one who would sanctify God's people. There, Jesus finds sheep who do hear his call, who put their trust in him.

Recall a recent discussion about faith with a non-Christian. What are the issues behind their questions and remarks? What do they need to hear and accept?

[1] Ezek 34:7 [2] Ps 82:6

BIBLE IN A YEAR: **Mark 16; Psalm 94**

Active Waiting

'Every morning I lay out the pieces of my life on your altar and watch for fire to descend.'[1]

Dear Thomas, when you say, 'Let us also go, that we may die with him' (v 16), I suspect I understand something of your confusion and compulsion about Jesus' ways. Even knowing what happens next, as I do, the poignant message from Martha and Mary to Jesus triggers so many memories of bad news meeting with a baffling response. The promise here that this story is not primarily about death sometimes sits uneasily next to grief so eloquently expressed in tears and longing and anger. Jesus' talk of sleeping and waking and dying gets tangled up in the realities of illness and loss, comfort and hope.

Thomas, what do you make of Jesus' attitude to time? His pace is unique. The plea from the sisters is not a demand to come, and yet when most would rush to the side of suffering friends, in *love* he delays the journey for two days. Are you relieved by the mention of Lazarus' restorative sleep, fearing danger and death for Jesus if he goes anywhere near Jerusalem? But then, when Jesus is ready to set off, you must feel that foreboding afresh in his sense of urgency. Those twelve hours of daylight he mentions focus on making the most of limited days. So how do you understand this movement between delay and deadline? In the future, when you look back, how will Jesus' surprising initial reaction to this crisis inform your growing understanding of him?

Is it Jesus' love which captivates you, Thomas? The deep affection that somehow mysteriously directs Jesus' puzzling response, both to linger and then to leave safety? Are you drawn to follow this man even to death, because you believe that being with him in his brilliance, even for a short time, is worth more than a lifetime in the dark without him? I get it, Thomas.

What do you think Jesus was doing during those two days? How might you honour him in your waiting?

[1] Ps 5:3, *The Message*

BIBLE IN A YEAR: **Ecclesiastes 1–3; 2 Thessalonians 2**

Gasp, Splutter and Blow

Take a moment to breathe. Breathe in God's tender love for you today. Breathe out your response to him.

Praise the Lord! You need breath to blow the trumpet with purposeful poise, to clash cymbals together with both arms, to shake a tambourine in rhythm, to hold a harp steady for delicate plucking. When you praise God, it is a whole-body offering of energy and eloquence. Imagine: today God's people in worship join the angels in their heavenly chorus. There is a collective gasp as the universe reverberates with exquisite harmony and unending melody.

Praise the Lord! He gifted you that breath as he kissed you into life. Each second, he does it again, whispering, 'Live! Fill your lungs, your blood vessels, your cells, your very bones with my life-giving oxygen. Inhale my goodness. Remember I am even closer to you than this breath pulsating through the marvellous, mortal body I crafted. As you exhale your praise, you are uniting with every creature across the planet and the centuries in adoration.'

Psalm 150 brings this biblical hymn book to a noisy, glorious finale. We have sung out our heartaches and hallelujahs, our anger and anguish, our pleading and petition, our questions and quandaries, our wonder and worship. The psalms reflect our evolving relationship with God throughout the years. They give full-bodied voice to our emotional responses as we live out our days in a wonderful, sin-scarred world. They express trust in our Creator, who saves and satisfies in abundance. Now, this has to be the last word, as our multifaceted experiences are all gathered up into one exuberant call: praise this matchless Lord of heaven and earth! Praise this God of mighty power and tender loving care! Grab any instrument and throw yourself into celebrating his greatness! Pour out your breath, all you have and all you are into jubilant song. Praise the Lord!

'... he breathed on them and said, "Receive the Holy Spirit."'[1] What does it mean to you today to have God's breath on you and in you?

[1] John 20:22

BIBLE IN A YEAR: **Ecclesiastes 4,5; 2 Thessalonians 3**

Plunging

'I do believe; help me overcome my unbelief!'[1] Come to Jesus as you are.

When someone you love dies, you are all over the place. Disbelief, exhaustion, regret, numbness, anger, disorientation, anguish and more all jostle amid the busyness and emptiness of the days which follow. Funeral rituals may provide some structure and a focus for the comforting gathering of family and friends, but the thoughts of 'if only' and 'I wish' lurk beneath the surface, sometimes tumbling out.

Grief comes to you; you cannot determine how it will be. The presence of Jesus, or what seems like his absence, is achingly significant. You may be unable to greet him, stuck sitting with people trying to be helpful, staring into a vacant future. Or you may go to him, pouring out your thoughts of 'if only', of rebuke or regret. At the same time, your faith can surprise you: perhaps declared with gritted-teeth conviction, or maybe with an assurance that surfaces unbidden.

This story of intimacy and grief unveils a space for you to enter. Here, close to the Mount of Olives, the prophets Joel[2] and Zechariah[3] envisaged a place of judgement and hope as God arrives at the end of time. Many were buried there, to be first at the end-times scene. Here, Jesus comes to be with Martha, to listen to her. He invites her to plunge deeper, past her vague belief in the resurrection of the dead on a last day, to grasp that resurrection and life are found in him now. While so much is still beyond her, her theology becomes personal, focused on Jesus: who he is and why he has come. Even as Lazarus is still dead, her heart encounters a revelation of the Son of God who has arrived at the Mount of Olives, ushering in new life and hope. She accepts the challenge to trust in him amid all the painful unknowns.

Is there someone bereaved – whether recently or longer term – to whom you can reach out? Bring them to Jesus in prayer.

[1] Mark 9:24 [2] Joel 2:32 [3] Zech 14:4

BIBLE IN A YEAR: **Ecclesiastes 6,7; Psalms 95,96**

John 11:32–44

Come and See

'Surely he took up our pain and bore our suffering ... he will see the light of life and be satisfied'.[1]

It's the sounds I notice first: the plaintive weeping of Mary as she throws herself at Jesus' feet. It's the wailing of the shuffling crowd who follow her, their Jewish duty and sympathy unwilling to leave her alone. Above all, it's the deep gutted sobbing of raw anguish and anger coming from Jesus. Hear the clamour of collective mourning, where one loss triggers memories of so many griefs. It was never meant to be this way. God in flesh enters fully – heart, voice and lungs – into the sorrow and suffering caused by Satan, sin and death.

Yet for those with eyes to see, there is glory. As the company move wretchedly to where Lazarus is laid, Jesus walks with purpose. Notice Martha's misery as she foresees the stench of decomposition now devouring her brother's body: 'No, Jesus, it really is not a good idea to have one last look. It's too late.' Watch the puzzlement as nonetheless the stone is rolled away

and everyone peers into the gloomy darkness. Imagine Jesus picturing his own future, the God-appointed hour soon to come, his vicarious, victorious self-giving response to the world's tragedy. There, before a baffled crowd of witnesses, a very dead man emerges by the life-giving power of God. While many miracles have been private, this one is very public: a sign pointing to God's presence and within reach of those who wish Jesus dead.

In the dazzling revelation of God, there is also an invitation. It comes in the shuffling figure of Lazarus, bound by the constraining cloths of burial. As we witness the ongoing work of the Spirit bringing spiritual life to those who dwell in the shadows, we are called to be involved with Jesus' work, to untie the cords of trauma and consequences of transgression. So the once-dead may be free indeed.

Pray for Christians you know who have been given a glorious new life in Christ, but need 'unwrapping' from grave clothes.

---

[1] Isa 53:4,11

BIBLE IN A YEAR: **Ecclesiastes 8,9; 1 Timothy 1**

John 11:45–57

For Good

**'You prepare a table before me in the presence of my enemies.'[1]
Come to the table.**

Recently I chatted online with two Christians living in countries where they are not free to worship openly. One has a surname which identifies him with another religion and he cannot legally convert. The other held up a scribbled text on paper, lest computer surveillance should alert the authorities to subversive language. As I listen, I am struck by parallels with our passage. Self-serving political and religious establishments have so much to gain by holding sway on the personal lives of others.

Jesus and his followers have enemies for all sorts of reasons. The same miraculous resurrection of Lazarus results both in believing and hardened hearts. The latter maliciously report to the religious authorities. Fearful of another imminent messianic revolt, the Sanhedrin convenes. Significantly, the fevered discussion is not, 'Who is this man? Is God in his actions?',

but 'How are we going to stop him? What if Rome responds by removing our power and privilege?' Expediency, cynicism and ugly boorishness from the high priest settle the matter: Jesus must die to preserve their vested interests. Innocence or guilt is inconsequential. Jerusalem residents and pilgrims must collaborate or be deemed accessories. The threat is chilling.

I pray that my persecuted friends will remember two things from this account. First, that their situations are held within the Father's sovereignty: Caiaphas' death wish is not a disaster. Rather, it is part of God's astonishing saving purpose. Second, that even though they may feel isolated, they belong to God's family. Jesus' death accomplished a global bringing together of people with one purpose: to love, serve, suffer and pray for his sake. Together, we live for him who never grasped power, but gave his life gladly for us.

Pray for brothers and sisters who suffer for Christ's sake, those you know and those dotted across the world.

[1] Ps 23:5

BIBLE IN A YEAR: **Ecclesiastes 10,11; 1 Timothy 2**

Tanya Ferdinandusz

HEARING THAT 'OTHER VOICE'

Tanya shares her journey to faith, the challenges of living through times of national political, economic and civil division, and the reassurance of God's presence in life's hardest moments.

Tanya, tell us a little about yourself.

I was born and have lived in Sri Lanka all my life. I've been married to Roshan for 30 years and we have two adult sons – Daniel and Joshua.

Growing up, I was nominally Christian. My relationship with Jesus began only as a young adult, after I started reading the Bible seriously for the first time. Through a year-long exploration of the Gospels, I came to know a Jesus whom I had never known before. No specific moment stands out as a conversion experience – I gradually grew into a conviction that Jesus is alive and that Christianity was true.

I worked as an accountant, but when my son was about a year old, I felt compelled to quit work to be a stay-home mum. As one door closed, the Lord opened a small window into the world of writing, a window that gradually broadened and also led me to Scripture Union. Many years later, God opened a door into the world of editing. Today, I enjoy the related but different work of both writing and editing.

Do you have a favourite section of Scripture? Why?

Yes, Genesis 1–3. Because I find these brief chapters are a treasure trove of life-transforming truths regarding the big questions about God, human life, the earth, marriage, work, sin... Without these foundational truths, we'd be left grappling with the way things are in a world gone so wrong; but these chapters

Tanya Ferdinandusz

reveal a Creator whose marvellous design is intended for our delight, whose wisdom knows best how life works best and whose love desires his best for us.

Was there a key person or event which helped you to start reading the Bible?

The 1980s were marked by civil unrest in Sri Lanka. In the late 1980s, my rejoicing over gaining entrance to university was short-lived because the universities remained closed, with a huge backlog of university entrants. While mourning this wasted time, I encountered a group called FOCUS (Fellowship of Christian University Students), who introduced me to Bible study. Prevented from studying law as I had planned, I spent a year taking my first baby steps in the study of God's law! – an experience that expanded not just my mind but also my heart, setting my feet on a life-path that I continue to walk today. One of the most crushing disappointments of my young life was thus transformed into a divine appointment that changed the course of my whole life!

How is the Bible part of your work and life today?

Since my work involves writing and editing Christian material, the Bible is essential core reading! Working with words has made me more keenly appreciative of the skilful word-craft of the biblical authors in conveying timeless truths so effectively and eloquently.

As for the Bible's place in my life, I can do no better than cite my favourite author, CS Lewis:

> All your wishes and hopes for the day rush at you like wild animals. And the first job each morning consists simply in shoving them all back; in listening to that other voice, taking that other point of view, letting that other, larger, stronger, quieter life come flowing in.[1]

Scripture is one key way in which I hear that 'other voice' above the clamour of many contradictory voices – a crucial corrective and one that often shapes my perspective for the day ahead before the day invades and takes over.

[1] CS Lewis, *Mere Christianity*, Macmillan, 1943, p169

Tanya Ferdinandusz

How do you read the Bible today?

For study purposes, when preparing for a talk or Bible study, I usually read larger blocks of Scripture, ask questions of the text, considering background and context and referring to dictionaries and commentaries. But for devotional reading, I find it necessary to shift gears from study mode to a more relational mindset. I've found that my best fit is to intentionally slow down to read, reflect and respond – this involves reading just a few verses (rather than long passages), spending time reflecting on phrases or ideas that resonate with me and then responding in prayer, sometimes writing down insights or prayers in a journal. Some of these thoughts find their way into what I write, become part of the Bible studies I lead or might be shared with a close friend.

Have there been key moments when the Word was a lifeline to you?

Almost ten years ago, I was on my way to collect a needle biopsy report. Desperate for assurance that nothing was wrong, my fingers searched on my phone for the familiar Psalm 91 – but Isaiah 43:2 popped up instead. I had absolutely no desire to hear about passing through deep waters or walking through fire! But those words God gave me in that moment were the words I needed as the lump was suspect and required surgery. With its assurance of God's presence come fire or water, this verse became the lifeline I clung to throughout surgery, recovery and in the weeks awaiting the results of the biopsy (it was benign).

While there have been a few such big moments, it's far more common for God to use his Word to bless me with timely reminders, gentle nudges or quiet affirmations. I find such moments hugely significant and comforting evidence of God's up-close-and-personal involvement in the details of the daily lives of ordinary people.

What has God spoken to you about most recently through the Bible?

In 2022, I was writing a series on Habakkuk for *Encounter with God* while Sri Lanka was plunged into an unprecedented political and economic crisis (which is still not over). The

Tanya Ferdinandusz

disconnect between Habakkuk's expectations of God and his experiences of God resonated with my own struggle, and I wrote:

> The raw edge of perplexed pain in the words tumbling off Habakkuk's tongue is my pain. The prophet's agonised struggle to make sense of God's apparent indifference ... and inaction ... is my struggle.

> Fears rise easily, while hope feels elusive, joy seems distant, and praise, quite frankly, is a struggle.

Most of what I wrote about in this series – Habakkuk's willingness to be real before God, his resolve to remain faithfully at his watch-post despite delays in God's response, his readiness to praise God even while all was not right with the world – felt like life-lessons being directed right back at me!

What has your Bible-journey been like?

I'm always 'still getting there', seldom moving as swiftly as I'd like to and, sometimes, just not moving at all!

For some time after those first baby steps thirty-odd years ago, my reading was confined mainly to the New Testament. Even when I first ventured into the Old Testament, I stayed with more manageable territory such as the Psalms and narratives such as Genesis or Exodus. But pursuing theological studies helped me to grasp the big story of Scripture and encouraged my exploration of the whole Bible (although history and geography have never been my strong points and I still struggle with some of the prophetic books).

My perspective on the Bible's purpose has changed – from viewing it primarily as a book that tells us how to live to experiencing it as a revelation and expression of God's heart for people. The title of this column reminds me that the way God's Word is 'a light to my path' is by being 'a lamp to my feet',[2] not illuminating the entire road ahead but casting a small circle of light around my feet – 'just enough light for the step I'm on'![3] A compelling reason to hold fast to that lamp and keep it close beside me so that, step by step, moment by moment, God might guide and lead me safely along his path of life.

[2] Ps 119:105, NRSV [3] Book title by Stormie Omartian, Harvest House, 1999

Scripture Union

A lasting legacy

· · · · · · · · · · · · · · · · ·

A gift in your Will can help put the good news into the hands and hearts of children and young people who don't go to church.

WRITING YOUR WILL?

Our FREE Will writing service can help!

Find out more:

🌐 su.org.uk/legacy

📞 01908 856120

'...we will tell the next generation the praiseworthy deeds of the Lord, his power, and the wonders he has done.' **Psalm 78:4**

Deuteronomy 16:18 – 34:12

LAWS FOR LIFE

'This day I call the heavens and the earth as witnesses against you that I have set before you life and death, blessings and curses. Now choose life, so that you and your children may live' (30:19). This verse summarises what Deuteronomy is all about. It is a kind of sermon, delivered just before his death by Moses to the Israelites as they prepared to enter Canaan. They should have possessed the land 38 years earlier, shortly after escaping from slavery in Egypt. Tragically, sinful rebellion against the Lord had earned them a life of wandering in the wilderness until that generation of rebels had died out. So Moses reminds them of their desert meanderings, concerned that they should not repeat the same mistakes but this time live in obedience to God.

Moses, because of his own disobedience to God, will not go with them (32:50–52). His successor, Joshua, whom some commentators credit with completing Deuteronomy after Moses' death, will lead them now. They know God's Law already. Poised to take possession of the Promised Land, they receive from Moses a recapitulation of it, with the Ten Commandments at its heart (5:1–22), which Moses develops in chapters 12–26. The book's name in English is taken from its title in the ancient Greek translation of the Old Testament known as the Septuagint – a combination of two Greek words: *deutero-* (second, meaning here a copy or repetition) and *nomos* (law).

Throughout Deuteronomy, we see Moses' passion for God's glory and his huge pastoral heart for God's people. It is such an important book that it is referenced extensively in the New Testament, notably by Jesus himself. Significantly, our Lord quotes it to refute the devil during his temptation in the desert.[1] In the same environment where the Israelites failed, he succeeds! Our examination of Deuteronomy 16–34 will be interspersed with a look at three psalms, two of which were penned by another man who, like Moses and Jesus, was a shepherd, King David.

Andrew Heron

[1] Matt 4:1–11; Luke 4:1–13

Law and Land

'How unsearchable [are God's] judgements, and his paths beyond tracing out!'[1]

The Lord here instructs Israel via Moses to establish a judicial system that will operate on two levels, local (lower courts) and national (high court). This God-given system must be entirely incorruptible and fair: even kings will not be above the Law (17:20); proof of guilt must be diligently sought (17:4); and capital punishment must not be administered on the testimony of one witness alone (17:6). The Israelites' possession and enjoyment of the land will depend wholly on their observance of these rules (16:20).

To many twenty-first-century readers, the sentences passed upon those proven guilty seem extremely harsh (17:5,12). However, we must note the safeguards that God puts in place to prevent miscarriages of justice (16:19; 17:6). We must also compare Israel's judicial system with that of its contemporary neighbours, for whom the law seems to have been anything but lenient or fair! Also, are we so sure that justice is uncorrupted and even-handed for everyone in the nations where we live today?

Israel's subsequent history shows that its people did not often wholly abide by the stipulations given here. Over and over again, God's laws were flouted by them, including by priests and kings! That they ever survived and are flourishing today is testimony to the truth stated by James, which ends with the gloriously comforting words, 'Mercy triumphs over judgment'.[2] Moreover, before we are tempted to point an accusing finger at the Israelites or anybody else, let us ask ourselves, 'Are we any better?' Therefore, if we catch ourselves being very quick to condemn others, remember Christ's words to the adulterous woman's would-be judges and jury, 'Let any one of you who is without sin be the first to throw a stone at her.'[3]

Think of ways to apply the dictum 'mercy triumphs over judgement' in your relationships!

---

[1] Rom 11:33 [2] James 2:12,13 [3] John 8:7

BIBLE IN A YEAR: **Ecclesiastes 12; 1 Timothy 3**

Heirs of God

Praise God for giving us himself in Christ!

The first section of today's text, verses 1–8, deals with the material provision Israel was to make for its ministers, the priests and Levites. These arrangements made sure that these men could look after the nation's spiritual welfare without worrying about where their next meal would come from. The same principle is rightly applied in most Christian churches for the support of their pastors and teachers. What a privilege Israel's priests and Levites enjoyed, to have the Lord as their sole inheritance (v 2). Since all Christ's followers together form 'a royal priesthood',[1] God himself has become our special inheritance too!

The second section, verses 9–13, speaks about the occult practices that prevailed in Canaan. God clearly hates human attempts to contact and harness the powers of the spiritual beings in the unseen realm. One of the most horrific rituals was the sacrifice of children as burnt offerings to the Canaanite deity, Molech. God must have a special place in his heart for 'little children', as witnessed by Jesus' tender words about them.[2] How much, then, should we Christians emulate our heavenly Father by cherishing and protecting the most vulnerable among us!

The third section, verses 14–22, warns Israel against false prophets, whose crime in leading people astray is so grave that it deserves the death penalty (v 20). They are easy to identify, because their messages fail to come true. Mankind's longing for truth and spiritual fulfilment leaves many open to abuse by self-seeking and often demon-inspired guides. Moses was a true prophet of God, but he points forward (v 15) to the coming of the Prophet of prophets to whom we must all listen – Jesus Christ. His voice is revealed and applied to us by his Spirit through the Scriptures.

Have you ever dabbled in the occult (eg horoscopes)? If so, have you been intentional in your renunciation of such practices?

[1] 1 Pet 2:9 [2] Matt 18:2–5

BIBLE IN A YEAR: **Song of Songs 1,2; Psalms 97,98**

Deuteronomy 19

Lex Talionis

Thank God that he has not given you what your sins deserve!

We return now to legal matters, to find God's prescriptions for the protection of the innocent and punishment of the guilty. Concerning the former, cities of refuge were to be designated, to which someone who had accidentally killed another could flee. There he was protected from the deceased's relatives (v 6), who could lawfully exact vengeance on a convicted murderer. These cities are a picture of God as refuge for his innocent people confronted with hate-filled enemies.[1] How much more amazing to think that Christ is a refuge for guilty sinners from the punishment their transgressions deserve!

Speaking of the guilty, our passage shows that, with God, crime does not pay! Be it murder (v 12), land theft (v 14) or false testimony in court (v 19), the punishment must match the crime, in accordance with the lex talionis – the law of retribution in kind (v 21). Retributive justice in most countries looks very different today. It usually involves a custodial sentence, though in some places the death penalty still exists. We might think the Old Testament's way was harsh, but remember – it was meant to prevent spiteful vengefulness, by setting precise limits on the punishments meted out.

Jesus appears to rescind this law.[2] Can he really be arguing against his own Word? Not so! The lex talionis was given to guide the judges in Israel's law courts. In its proper context, maybe we should consider whether the principle has some value for us today. In contrast, Jesus is thinking of personal relationships. He is forbidding us from seeking revenge on someone who has slighted us personally. Rather, we must treat that person with unwarranted kindness – a theme we see Paul develop.[3]

Pray for the judiciary in your country, that justice and mercy may be implemented in a balanced way that will, whether intentionally or instinctively, uphold biblical principles!

[1] Pss 46:1; 18:2 [2] Matt 5:38,39 [3] Rom 12:19–21

BIBLE IN A YEAR: **Song of Songs 3,4; 1 Timothy 4**

The Key to Happiness

Lord, please help me to understand how much my happiness depends on the cultivation of holiness in my life!

The patriarch Jacob's eighth son was born to Zilpah, his wife Leah's handmaid. Leah was so delighted she called the baby 'Asher', meaning 'happy' in Hebrew.[1] In Psalm 127:5, the same word is translated 'blessed' in many English Bibles, in reference to the happiness of the man who has many children! Well, God takes great delight in his children and desires for them blessing and happiness too. So he tells us how to acquire it – by living according to his Word! This is what Psalm 1 is all about.

The psalm opens with a word that shares the same Hebrew root as the name 'Asher'. It teaches that true happiness comes through faithful obedience to God's 'law' (v 2). That 'law' is not seen as a heavy burden weighing people down, nor as a set of kill-joy rules and regulations meant to make life miserable. On the contrary, it fills the righteous with such delight that they think on it constantly (v 2). They pay heed to its warnings and avoid going along with the unrighteous crowd that wilfully disregards it (v 1). That's why their lives resemble a strong, well-watered fruit tree (v 3), whereas the wicked are blown away like the dry, scaly casing of cereal grains after threshing (v 4). Real contentment is found in God alone. Rejecting him only leads to disaster.

Many times throughout Deuteronomy, which we are studying together these next few weeks, God urges Israel to obey his laws 'so that it may go well with you'.[2] Obedience and well-being are inextricably linked. This is what Psalm 1 makes abundantly clear. Knowing and loving God's Word is the key to happiness. So, let's read it, enjoy it and not make a chore out of it!

Today, even though your heart may be hurting badly, try counting your blessings to see what God has done!

[1] Gen 30:12,13 [2] Eg Deut 4:40; 12:25; 19:13; 22:7

BIBLE IN A YEAR: **Song of Songs 5,6; 1 Timothy 5**

Deuteronomy 20

Rules for War

Pray for help to leave in God's hands some aspects from today's reading you might find difficult to accept or understand.

War is the subject of today's reading. The main section deals with ordinary wars, ie with enemies other than the wicked inhabitants of Canaan. Israel's conduct in war was to be more humane than that of its neighbours. For instance, exemption from fighting was allowed for various reasons, including fear (v 8)! Peaceful surrender was preferable to killing (vs 10–15). Fruit trees must not be senselessly destroyed (v 19).

Priestly involvement in war (vs 2–4) reminds us that Israel was a theocracy. In biblical understanding, no other nation has ever been in that category. Even so, many belligerents claim that God is on their side. As Lord of the nations, he certainly champions the triumph of good over evil, but we must beware of letting narrow nationalistic interests define good and evil! In the light of war's inevitable ugliness, some Christians choose to be pacifists or conscientious objectors. We all must decide in accordance with the guidance we have sought from God on this matter, and avoid judging each other.

The command to completely annihilate the people living in Canaan (vs 16–18) comes as a shock to modern sensitivities. It causes many to reject the Bible outright and others to believe the Old and New Testaments speak of two different Gods. Many of the Deuteronomic laws were given to prevent Israel from following 'all the detestable things [the Canaanites] do in worshipping their gods' (v 18). Behind these 'gods' were demonic entities whose worship demanded the worst human depravities imaginable. They had to be stopped! A clearer grasp of God's absolute holiness can help our understanding here. Remember also, our eyes do not fully discern the ferocity and intensity of the cosmic spiritual warfare raging around us.

Ask God to hasten the day when war will cease. Pray for its victims around the world at this time.

BIBLE IN A YEAR: **Song of Songs 7,8; Psalms 99–101**

Atoning Grace

Heavenly Father, please teach me to be gracious, like you.

The unlawful killing of a person made in the image of God greatly angers the Giver of life. Therefore, murder defiled the land and made cleansing necessary. The provisions mentioned here were intended to clear the inhabitants of the town nearest the murder scene from 'the guilt of shedding innocent blood' (v 9). Guilt for such wrongdoing is so serious that only blood sacrifice can turn away God's righteous anger, whether the perpetrator can be identified or not. Ultimately, God dealt with the guilt of our wrongdoing through the sacrifice of himself in Christ. That's a measure of how sinful our sins are, including those of which we are unaware. It's also a measure of how amazing God's grace is!

That grace extends to providing protection for foreign women taken captive in war and firstborn sons at risk of being disinherited (vs 10–17). In these matters, God insists on fair treatment among his people for the vulnerable. How much do we imitate our heavenly Father by standing with the vulnerable in society to defend and protect them?

However, such displays of divine grace are negated in many people's opinion by the closing stipulation in today's passage. Parents are instructed on how they must discipline their profligate sons. Have them stoned to death? Seriously? The Bible records no example of this ever actually happening. Nonetheless, it comes as a shock! This law was quite likely to have been meant to serve as a deterrent against reckless, decadent behaviour and an incentive to godly, disciplined child-rearing. Social order depended on strong, healthy familial ties. Many Christians believe that society is breaking down today because of a concerted attack on traditional family values. Who can prove them wrong?

Pray for parents struggling to bring up young children and teenagers in the ways of the Lord in today's ultra-permissive world.

BIBLE IN A YEAR: Isaiah 1,2; 1 Timothy 6

Dare to be Different

Lord, let me not be so heavenly minded as to be of no earthly good!

Here we find various laws for dealing humanely with the corpses of executed criminals, encouraging good neighbourliness, respecting gender distinctions, providing safety regulations for buildings, promoting animal welfare and protecting the sanctity of marriage. These are more or less self-explanatory. However, the four laws given in verses 9–12 are a bit of a surprise! Why were the Israelites forbidden from planting two different kinds of seed in a vineyard, yoking together two different kinds of animals for ploughing and wearing clothes made of mixed fibres? And what's this about adding tassels to their cloaks?

A clue to solving the mystery can be found in Numbers 15:37–41. These verses explain that the tassels on garments were given as a visual aid to remind the Israelites about the Lord's commandments. Obedience to those commandments marked Israel out as God's unique people. It has been suggested that the forbidden combinations may have been pagan customs the Canaanites used to invoke the blessing of their false gods. Whatever the precise explanation, it seems safe to assume that, as with the tassels, their prohibition too was to be a mark of Israel's distinctiveness.

These laws, then, present Christians today with the spiritual principle of separation. We are not required to implement the laws themselves. However, just as God desired to keep Israel separate, so too Jesus' followers must maintain spiritual separation from the sinful practices all around us. As with Deuteronomy's ploughing animals, we must not be 'yoked together with unbelievers'.[1] However, in struggling to live in the world but not of it, let's remember that we should be a redemptive presence in the place and among the people where God has put us!

Think through what avoiding being 'yoked together with unbelievers' might mean for you.

[1] 2 Cor 6:14

BIBLE IN A YEAR: **Isaiah 3–5; 2 Timothy 1**

Sheep and Goats

'... broad is the road that leads to destruction ... and narrow the road that leads to life'.[1]

Today's reading describes people forbidden from entering 'the assembly [*qahal*] of the LORD' (vs 1,3). The exact meaning of this term is debatable. However, the prohibition clearly rendered full participation in the life of the community impossible for the excluded. In light of today's emphasis on inclusivity, it seems cruel to discriminate on the basis of physical deformity, illegitimate birth or foreign extraction. If all people are created equally in the image of God, how could God bar certain types of individual from integration into the Israelite community?

Well, throughout Deuteronomy, the Israelites are commanded to be different from the neighbouring nations. Several times already in the book of Leviticus, God had commanded them, 'be holy, because I am holy'.[2] 'Holiness' basically signifies 'otherness'. God himself is wholly other, so his people must not treat him flippantly

and with presumptuous overfamiliarity. As his representatives on earth, they must be wholly other too. Therefore, God imposes certain standards that we today might find unfair, but were intended to maintain Israel's national uniqueness.

In the Septuagint, an ancient Greek translation of the Old Testament, *qahal* is often translated using the word *ekklesia*. This means literally 'a called-out assembly'. In the New Testament, this is commonly translated as 'church'. Christians desire to be as inclusive as possible. Nevertheless, we must remember that the assembly of God's true people consists exclusively of those who have faith in Jesus. Christ's analogy of the sheep and goats[3] illustrates how mankind will ultimately be divided into two categories, based on what is done (or left undone) for him. Nothing keeps anyone out of Christ's redeemed community except refusal to believe in him.

Ask God for opportunities this week to present the way of salvation to people around you who do not know Jesus.

[1] Matt 7:13,14 [2] Eg Lev 11:44 [3] Matt 25:31–46

BIBLE IN A YEAR: **Isaiah 6,7; 2 Timothy 2**

Deuteronomy 24:10 – 25:19

God-Talk and God-Acts

Pray that the faith you profess will be reflected in the life you lead.

The Hebrew word for faith, *emunah*, also means 'faithfulness'. For the Israelites, trust in God involved correct belief about God, which issued in right living for him. Active obedience to his commands, of which we find many once again in today's passage, was the supreme test of faith. It mattered little how well you knew God's commands if you totally failed to live by them. Deuteronomy 12:28 gives a beautiful summary of what faith/faithfulness entailed for the Hebrews and how it was meant to benefit them and also to honour the Lord.

Among the various commands we read today is one that requires merciful treatment for foreigners, orphans and widows (24:17,18). For James, this kind of positive action is precisely what constitutes true religion for Christian followers of Jesus.[1] There we find the Hebraic insistence that faith must entail faithfulness (obedient action). In case we miss his point, James further defines faith,[2] wonderfully conveyed by *The Message* version: 'Isn't it obvious that God-talk without God-acts is outrageous nonsense?'

When defining their faith, Christians often begin by referring to what they believe about Jesus. Certainly, a true Christian cannot hold erroneous beliefs about our Lord. As Deuteronomy shows, however, trusting God is more than mere intellectual assent to creeds or systematic theologies. Interestingly, the New Testament Greek word for faith, *pistis*, like its Hebrew equivalent, also conveys the notion of 'faithfulness'. That means that genuine Christian faith is eminently practical. It demands that a professing believer's right thinking about Jesus is fleshed out in right living based on biblical teaching. Our lives may be the only Bible many people ever read!

Whenever you read the Bible, ask yourself: how does the passage before you inform what you believe and provide you with guidelines by which to live?

[1] James 1:27 [2] James 2:17

BIBLE IN A YEAR: **Isaiah 8,9; Psalm 102**

Remember! Remember!

'Praise the Lord, my soul, and forget not all his benefits'.[1]

We come now to the end of the section that began in chapter 12 and deals with specific legislation. Stipulations are given for the offering of the first fruits and third-year tithes. The first fruits were a foretaste of the full harvest to come. In the New Testament, believers are the first fruits, saved to bear fruit for God in the here and now.[2] We have also received the 'firstfruits of the Spirit' as a foretaste here and now of what will come in the afterlife.[3]

While offering the first fruits, the Israelite worshipper was to recite verses 5–10, which summarise God's gracious acts on his people's behalf. Starting with Jacob, the patriarch who gave Israel its name, the passage ends with the Israelites arriving in the Promised Land after being freed from Egyptian bondage. Some regard these verses as a kind of early Israelite creed. Significantly, they are recited as part of the traditional Jewish Passover celebration.

Remembering how God helped us in the past wonderfully encourages us to trust him both in the present and in the future. Some Christians record in a journal what the Lord has done for them. Others cherish in their hearts memories of special times when he protected and blessed them. We have a powerful visual aid to remind us of the historical event that changed for ever the lives of all who follow Jesus – the bread and wine of Communion! These help us never to forget what Christ did for us at the cross. The firstfruits ritual was intended as a joyful celebration. Communion for Christians should never resemble a funeral service. It certainly focuses on Christ's sacrificial death, but it urges us to rejoice that Christ is risen and will come again![4]

Give thanks that Jesus has left us a wonderful memorial meal in Communion, which looks both backwards and forwards.

[1] Ps 103:2 [2] 2 Thess 2:13 [3] Rom 8:23 [4] 1 Cor 11:26

BIBLE IN A YEAR: **Isaiah 10–12; 2 Timothy 3**

Psalm 3

Arise, Lord!

Lord, let me not be overcome by evil, but help me overcome evil with good.[1]

The events surrounding the writing of Psalm 3 (David's flight from Absalom) are related in 2 Samuel 15–18. The king has to contend not only with the personal grief of his own son's rebellion, but also with the disloyalty of many who sided with Absalom (vs 1,6) and their taunt that God has abandoned him (v 2). Yet, his hope is in the Lord, who will protect, answer and rescue him (vs 3,4,7,8). He is so confident of divine intervention that he can sleep peacefully in the knowledge of God's sustaining presence (v 5).

This psalm is not usually counted as one of the imprecatory psalms,[2] in which the writer invokes the Lord's curse of judgement or destruction upon his enemies. Nevertheless, verse 7 sounds very similar to these. David pictures his enemies almost animalistically, like ferocious beasts poised to devour him, whose ravenous attack can only be thwarted by a knock-out blow from God. Maybe he had in mind the bear and the lion God had saved him from as a shepherd boy.[3] How should Christians feel about such vengeful language this side of Jesus' command to love and pray for our enemies?[4]

Well, David's words certainly sound harsh to our ears. But remember that he and God's people faced the constant threat of destruction by many enemies. So notice here that he does not talk of avenging his foes himself, but is content to commit them to God's justice. Their judgement and destruction are left in the Lord's capable hands! From this, Christians can learn that we can trust God to enact his justice on those who persecute us for Christ's sake, while praying for them to repent before they have to face divine judgement.

Look up Romans 12:19 and learn the verse by heart!

---

[1] Prayer based on Rom 12:21 [2] Eg Pss 5,10,17,35 [3] 1 Sam 17:37 [4] Matt 5:43,44

BIBLE IN A YEAR: **Isaiah 13,14; 2 Timothy 4**

Break One, Break All!

Father, please cover with the blood of Jesus and forgive the sins I have committed and of which I am ignorant.

Instructions are given to the Israelites, in today's reading, about a dramatic ceremony for ratifying their covenant with God after they enter Canaan. By publicly pronouncing curses on themselves for breaches of the Law, followed by loud amens, they would express agreement with whatever penalties God would impose for disobedience. These penalties, as well as blessings for obedience, are itemised in detail in chapters 28 and 29.

The final curse mentioned in verse 26 does not refer to the violation of any particular command, but to any breach of the Law in general. In the New Testament, James picks up on the same idea by stating that 'whoever keeps the whole law and yet stumbles at just one point is guilty of breaking all of it.'[1] Thus every single one of us is a law-breaker for, in spite of our best efforts, we will never be able to obey God's commands perfectly and at all times.

The apostle Paul quotes verse 26 to explain that trying to gain acceptance with God by relying on our own obedience to the Law is doomed to failure.[2] Quite simply, the Law can only show us our shortcomings. It has no power to help us overcome them. Like a mirror, it reveals what we look like but it cannot change our appearance. That is why God gave Israel a sacrificial system, whereby national and individual sins were forgiven exclusively through the blood of animals offered in substitution for the repentant sinner. These sacrifices had to be repeated over and over again. A permanent solution was needed. It came in the form of Jesus Christ, who was able to keep the Law perfectly and bear the curse for humanity! Have you trusted in him as your substitute?

Praise God for the gift of Jesus Christ, who bears our sins for us and sets us free.

[1] James 2:10 [2] Gal 3:10

BIBLE IN A YEAR: Isaiah 15,16; Psalm 103

Deuteronomy 28:1–14

Walking with God

Heavenly Father, thank you for the blessings with which you fill my life.

Sometimes we make someone a generous promise, demanding nothing in return. God does that too. For example, after the flood, he promised unconditionally never again to curse the ground because of man;[1] he promised unconditionally never again to destroy all creatures by a flood.[2] However, just like ours, God's promises sometimes depend on certain requirements being met for their fulfilment. The blessings promised to Israel in today's reading are of that kind. Four times obedience is mentioned as the condition for their bestowal (vs 1,2,9,13).

First, let us consider what it means to 'walk in obedience' to God (v 9). When we arrange a walk with a close friend, it is because we enjoy their company and the opportunity to chat and share what is on our hearts. Well, God loves fellowship with us. Walking with him is like holding a two-way conversation by which we hear his voice through his Word and by his Spirit, and speak to him in prayer. The more we get to know him, the more we choose to obey him, not under compulsion but because of love. Israel failed to understand this. Do we fare any better?

Second, note that God's blessings on Israel were meant to be a testimony to all nations, an example of what happens when a people obediently follows the true and living God (v 10). That was intended as a means of drawing the nations to God, that they might be blessed too. God had promised this to Abraham, Israel's forefather, many centuries earlier.[3] Ultimately, that blessing took the form of the Messiah's coming into the world for our salvation. He saved us, that we might draw others to him.

Cleopas and another disciple walked and talked with Jesus on the road to Emmaus.[4] What would you have asked him if you had been there?

---

[1] Gen 8:20,21 [2] Gen 9:11 [3] Gen 12:3; 22:18 [4] Luke 24

BIBLE IN A YEAR: **Isaiah 17–20; Titus 1**

The Awe-Inspiring God

Lord, I am often fickle and faint-hearted. Please keep me faithful to the very end!

The curses for disobedience here are almost overwhelming. They are intended as a deterrent. Israel should have realised that it must avoid flouting the divine law at all costs. Tragically, not long after settling in Canaan, the people began sinning so grievously that God would have to keep his word and judge them severely. Eventually, that meant being cast out of the land altogether – in 722 BC (the northern kingdom, Israel) and 605–586 BC (the southern kingdom, Judah). A remnant of Jews returned to Judah around 538 BC, but the Romans totally dispersed them in AD 70, as verse 64 foretold.

People today, including many Christians, find it hard to accept that a loving God could punish so harshly. Perhaps that comes from a failure to understand God's absolute holiness. He unequivocally warns the Israelites in verse 58 to revere his 'glorious and awesome name' or face the consequences. Nowadays, the adjective 'awesome' is so overused, we scarcely remember that 'awe' originally had to do with fear or dread. In the New Testament, the writer to the Hebrews conveys something of what 'awe' is all about: 'It is a dreadful thing to fall into the hands of the living God.'[1]

There is a sobering message from today's reading for the church. Like Israel of old (v 9), we are called 'a holy nation'.[2] We are meant to display God's glory and goodness in the world. If we fail to do so, we can expect to be disciplined as Israel was.[3] Faithful endurance to the very end is required of us,[4] unless we want to avoid being cut off like Israel.[5] Let us not ignore the warnings!

'The fear of the Lord is the beginning of wisdom'.[6] How is that 'fear' reflected in your life and in your church?

[1] Heb 10:31 [2] 1 Pet 2:9 [3] Heb 12:4–11 [4] Matt 10:22; 24:13; Heb 10:36; 2 Tim 2:12 [5] Rom 11:20–22 [6] Ps 111:10

BIBLE IN A YEAR: **Isaiah 21,22; Titus 2**

Deuteronomy 29

No Trespassing

Thank you, Father, for revealing to us everything we need to know to be saved.

God's covenant with Israel, made 40 years earlier at Horeb, is now reconfirmed with a new generation of Israelites, before they enter the Promised Land. Moses urges them once again to keep the covenant and thus avoid the dire consequences that arise from breaking it. Could God have explained things any more plainly? It is hard to imagine so, yet the lure of sin would prove stronger than Israel's commitment to remain faithful to him. We all know something about that, don't we?

Speaking of knowledge, God makes it abundantly clear to the Israelites in verse 29 that they and, by extension, we have received absolutely everything we need for understanding why and how we must obey the Lord. Revelation is the process by which God shows us truths it would otherwise be impossible for us to discover. Those truths are preserved in written form in the Bible, so that the divine message can be heard and transmitted from generation to generation. The importance of Scripture for teaching us to live in the way that pleases God cannot be exaggerated.

Nevertheless, God has placed limits on what is revealed to us. '… all the words of this law' (v 29) are given to guide our path but they do not include knowledge that God has deliberately put beyond our reach. Much that happens in the unseen spiritual realm is kept from us. To delve too deeply into such things can lead us into the forbidden zone of occultism (from Latin *occultus* – hidden). God expressly prohibits this throughout Scripture.[1] The very first temptation was an enticement to know as God knows.[2] Eve's story and verse 29 in today's reading warn us against trespassing on forbidden territory.

If you haven't already done so, consider reading the whole Bible through in one year and getting an overall grasp of God's revelation.

[1] Eg Lev 19:31; 20:6,27; Isa 8:19; 2 Kings 21:6; Acts 19:19; Rev 21:8 [2] Gen 3:4,5

BIBLE IN A YEAR: **Isaiah 23,24; Titus 3**

Take it, Don't Leave it!

Lord, thank you that you do not force me but you do want me to choose life rather than death.

What an abundantly rich passage today's reading is! Verses 1–10 contain promises of restoration for Israel after it has repented from what is suggested will be its inevitable fall. There is also clarification that a right relationship with God is based not on outward ritualism but on inner conviction by way of a transformed (circumcised) heart. Verses 11–20 show that keeping the covenant with God is not an impossible task – and they end with Moses' exhortation to make the right choice. The apostle Paul quotes from this chapter, summing it up by stating that faith in Jesus Christ is the fulfilment of all that Moses says for both Jew and Gentile.[1]

Moses' plea about choosing rightly teaches us that God does not force his will on anyone. He made us in his image. We are able therefore to think consciously with our mind, feel with our heart and decide with our will. We were not created to be robots. However, since the fall, all of mankind struggles to make the right choices because of our sinful nature. Praise God, he has made his Word available to us for our guidance. We joyfully thank him for that – but are we concerned to share his Word with those who do not know it yet?

One final thought. Can you sense Moses' passion as he pleads with Israel to choose life over death? We detect no indifferent 'take it or leave it' attitude here. Behind his passion, we feel the loving heart of God beating with the same compassion Jesus displayed when he saw the crowds 'harassed and helpless' in the places where he preached.[2] Oh, that the fires of such passion/compassion were kindled more often in our pulpits, urging people to make the right choices in life!

Ask God to renew your passion to pray for those you love who do not yet know Jesus.

[1] Rom 10:5–13 [2] Matt 9:36

BIBLE IN A YEAR: **Isaiah 25,26; Psalm 104**

Deuteronomy 31:1–29

God-Confidence

Lord, sometimes my heart is more like a mouse's than a lion's. Increase my courage to be bold for you!

'When I come out, I have supreme confidence. But I'm scared to death.'[1] These words were spoken, surprisingly, by 'Iron Mike' Tyson, world heavyweight boxing champion from 1987 to 1990. How could such a fearsome man be frightened of anything? Maybe in the end even the apparently superhuman are just like the rest of us mere mortals! Isn't that reassuring?

We probably think of Joshua, Moses' successor, as some kind of fearless warrior whose example we could never emulate. He is certainly one of the Bible's great heroes. Born a slave in Egypt, he was one of only two adult men of his generation (the other being Caleb) to enter the Promised Land. Both had been among the 12 spies sent out 38 years earlier to reconnoitre the land. They alone urged an immediate invasion – and God honoured them for it.

Joshua became Moses' special assistant during the wilderness wanderings, then later led Israel to victory over its fierce Amalekite enemies. Here was someone eminently qualified to command Israel in their conquest of Canaan. We rightly admire his achievements!

Yet, three times in Deuteronomy 31 (vs 7,8,23) and three times in Joshua 1 (vs 6,7,9), God had to tell him to be strong, courageous and unafraid. Does this not indicate that, deep down, he was not so brave after all? Perhaps! But, more importantly, it shows where he got the confidence to accomplish his great exploits – from his trust in the Lord who equipped and sent him! Born 'Hoshea' but called 'Joshua' by Moses,[2] how well he bore that name, which means 'the Lord is salvation!' Our faith may seem small, but if it is in a great God, that's all that matters!

Christian biographies often portray their subject with a superhero gloss. Compare this with the Bible's portrayal of its heroes like Abraham, Moses and David!

[1] https://casnocha.com/2009/06/im-scared-to-death-but-supremely-confident.html [2] Num 13:16

BIBLE IN A YEAR: **Isaiah 27,28; Philemon**

Covenant Benefits

Take time to praise the Lord for his promise, based on his covenant with you, never to leave or forsake you.

Last Sunday, we saw King David in Psalm 3 calling upon God to destroy his enemies. He committed their punishment to the Lord, in keeping with Deuteronomy 32:35 and 36. In today's reading, the king again needs rescuing from his foes, but his appeal to God is somewhat different this time. As verses 1 and 3 indicate, it is based on his covenant relationship as a 'godly' (literal meaning of 'faithful' in verse 3) man with the merciful God who justifies his people.

Many English versions of verse 1, following the original Hebrew and its ancient Greek translation (Septuagint), have David addressing the Lord as the 'God of my righteousness'. This conveys the idea that God alone is just (righteous) and the justifier of those who trust in him – a notion taken up in the New Testament by the apostle Paul (see below). David here underlines his spiritual dependency on God. He is not righteous in himself, but solely because of God's compassion towards him. That is why he cries to God, 'have mercy on me' (v 1). He doesn't deserve God's help, but expects it on the basis of his Vindicator's covenant love.

All of this prefigures the relationship between Christians and Christ. By accepting that he died in our place (as our substitute), taking the punishment our sins deserve, we are declared not guilty in the divine court where our Judge is the only one who can justify us.[1] King David understood the essentials, though not the particulars, of this glorious truth. For Christians, the 'sacrifices' and 'trust' he mentions in verse 5 are centred on Christ. Because we have entered into the new covenant in his blood,[2] we, like David, can enjoy God's peace and expect God's help for his own name's sake.

By using a concordance (or internet), learn about the Bible's five foundational covenants which involved Abraham, Noah, Moses, David and Jesus.

[1] Rom 3:25,26 [2] 1 Cor 11:25

BIBLE IN A YEAR: **Isaiah 29,30; Hebrews 1**

Deuteronomy 31:30 – 32:47

A Rock Anthem

Before today's meditation, read or sing a hymn of praise that focuses on God's greatness!

It has been said that most Christians get their theology from their hymns rather than from preachers' sermons! One of the best ways to memorise something is to put it to music. So God knew what he was doing when he instructed Moses to write this song and teach it to Israel (31:19). Few songs are as full of significant messaging as this one. Committing it to memory was vital for Israel, for these 'are not just idle words for you – they are your life' (32:47).

Moses' song succinctly recalls Israel's history and gives prophetic warnings against the danger of idolatry that leads to apostasy and judgement. It also promises vengeance against the enemies of God and of his people, emphasising God's faithfulness to his chosen nation. This musical composition is a model for our congregational hymns. They may not be divinely inspired like this one, but they should preferably be soaked in Scriptural truth and set to memorable, simple tunes.

Moses' song might be called the world's first rock anthem, but not the kind with soaring guitars, pounding drums and throbbing basses. Rather, it repeatedly calls God the Rock (vs 4,15,18,30,31). 'Rock' translates the Hebrew word *'tzur'*, which denotes a block of stone, a boulder or a cliff. It came to be associated with the idea of refuge and appears as such throughout the Old Testament, most notably in the Psalms.[1] Its use by Moses encouraged the Israelites not to stray from the Lord but always to abide faithfully in the protective shadow of his presence, for he is the only foundation for a stable life. According to Jesus, hearing and implementing his words is acting like a wise man who built his house on the rock.[2] Now there's something to sing about!

Read or sing out loud your favourite Christian hymn or song, then transform it into a prayer of praise to God using your own words!

---

[1] Pss 62:7; 78:35; 144:1 [2] Matt 7:24–27

BIBLE IN A YEAR: Isaiah 31,32; Psalm 105

Deuteronomy 32:48 – 33:29

Sin's Consequences

Father, let me neither despair over my failings nor take your forgiveness for granted.

Our passage explains why God barred Moses from entering Canaan. At Meribah, God told Moses to provide the Israelites with water from a rock by speaking to it. Instead, Moses struck it, thus dishonouring the Lord before the people.[1] His disobedience did not cut him off from God's presence, but he lost the privilege of leading the people into the Promised Land. Sin in a believer's life is forgiven after repentance, but it can still leave serious consequences!

Sin's consequences might also be alluded to with regard to an important omission in Moses' blessing from today's reading. Every tribe is blessed individually, except Simeon. Many Bible commentators believe this has to do with Jacob's condemnation of Simeon and Levi and his promise that they will be scattered among their brothers for avenging their sister Dinah's rape when they killed the men of Shechem.[2] Levi was indeed scattered among the other tribes and no territory was allotted to them apart from some cities. Nevertheless, Moses blesses them, probably because they redeemed their reputation in the golden calf episode and by Aaron's family's role in the Baal of Peor incident.[3] What, then, about Simeon?

Simeon did receive an inheritance in Israel, but only a portion in the territory that was allotted to Judah.[4] It appears that they were absorbed into Judah – though some may have migrated to the northern kingdom of Israel after the schism. However, they are rarely mentioned as a separate entity after the settlement of Canaan and they do not figure much in Jewish rabbinical literature. Let us all take note: repentance brings full and free forgiveness, but sin's consequences may still be severe.

In recent years, the sins of many prominent Christian leaders have been exposed and God's name dishonoured. Pray that they will genuinely repent and be restored.

[1] Num 20:1–13 [2] Gen 49:5–7; 34 [3] Exod 32:25–29; Num 25:1–14 [4] Josh 19:1–9

BIBLE IN A YEAR: **Isaiah 33,34; Hebrews 2**

Deuteronomy 34

Prophet of Prophets!

Triune God, Father, Son and Holy Spirit, teach me to worship only you, for you alone are worthy!

Here ends the story of one of history's most significant figures. Well, not quite (see below)! The account of Moses' death was obviously written by someone other than the great man himself. Perhaps it was the same person (possibly Joshua?) who says that Moses was the humblest man on earth.[1] How amazing that, for all the mighty acts God accomplished through him (vs 10–12), he remained extremely modest. Christian leaders would do well to take a leaf out of his book!

The Israelites lamented Moses' death for 30 days (v 8) before proceeding into Canaan under Joshua's leadership. We are given a very interesting detail about his funeral arrangements – God kept his burial place hidden (v 6)! Imagine how, if the site of his grave had been public knowledge, it could easily have become a place of veneration drawing thousands of pilgrims. Believers are often tempted to idolise great men and women of God rather than give all the glory to the Lord they served.

Let us note two things in closing. First, as we rightly praise God for the superlative prophet Moses was (v 10), let us rejoice that he was superseded by the ultimate Prophet of whom all others were types and shadows, our Lord Jesus Christ! Second, Moses makes one more appearance in Scripture after his death – on the mount of transfiguration. There he converses with the Messiah in all his glory, along with Elijah.[2] Just think – one day, all Christ's followers will contemplate the divine countenance, as Moses and Elijah did!

Deuteronomy ends with the Israelites about to enter Canaan. Meditate on the Promised Land that awaits us.[3]

[1] Num 12:3 [2] Matt 17:1–8 [3] Rev 21:1–5

BIBLE IN A YEAR: **Isaiah 35,36; Hebrews 3**

A SHEPHERD'S WARNING

Jude is rather off-putting, to put it mildly! His language seems extremely negative. A huge stumbling block for many is Jude's obscure references to Moses, the Archangel Michael and Balaam. We can just about understand his point about Sodom and Gomorrah, but where does the Old Testament talk about the body of Moses?! Jude refers to other Jewish texts that are unfamiliar to us: 1 Enoch – which is not even included in the Apocrypha – develops the story about the fallen angels in Genesis 6 ('sons of God', Genesis 6:2); 1 Enoch also has a 'Book of Dreams' that Jude and the apostates may both have read. A Jewish text called the Testament of Moses – much of which is lost to church history – could have been Jude's source for his argument about the body of Moses (v 9).[1] A study Bible or a good commentary will help to explain some of the more obscure references, or you can read 1 Enoch yourself to get a better understanding of the apocalyptic texts that the early church were familiar with.

It's clear from the New Testament that the believers wrestled with these texts and were sometimes pulled away from the apostles' teaching by interpretations of texts like 1 Enoch. Jude knows the mystical teaching as well as the false teachers do, but he is not lured away from the revelation of the Lord Jesus Christ and the apostles' teaching.

Jude is often found as a companion to 2 Peter in commentaries. There are strong links between Jude and 2 Peter 2 and 3, both in language and message. It is unclear who borrowed from whom: Jude 17 and 18 refer to the apostles' teaching, a seeming reference to 2 Peter 3:3.[2] Both Peter's and Jude's letters reveal the Shepherd's protective love; both deliver a strong but loving warning to God's holy people about false teaching and falling away. This is still a vital message for us today, as we will see over the next two days.

Katharine McPhail

---

[1] Richard J Bauckham, *Jude, 2 Peter*, Word, 1983, p74–76 [2] Douglas Moo, 'Introduction to 2 Peter and Jude', *2 Peter and Jude*, ebook.

Jude 1–16

Lord, have Mercy

'To him who is able to keep you from stumbling ... to the only God our Saviour be glory, majesty, power and authority, through Jesus Christ our Lord' (vs 24,25).

Jude's language about false teachers and evil influencers in the church is very strong, but so is his affirming language towards believers. They are 'called ... loved ... and kept' by the Father for the Lord Jesus (v 1). God holds them safe in loving, eternal security. They are God's holy ones, to whom God has entrusted the faith (v 3). Not only can we trust God completely, but God trusts us with the true message of salvation. Jude contrasts this dramatically with the fate of the false teachers – ungodly, immoral, devious and under the condemnation of God (v 4) – kept for destruction. Jude identifies the greatest double danger to the believers: the perversion of the teaching about grace and the denial that Jesus Christ is Lord. Both lead to destruction, as he so vividly describes.

Jude is distressed that the believers have not recognised this attack on the church and the lordship of Christ. The clarity of the gospel message and the history of God's people (vs 5–11) should have been enough to show them the danger, but he realises that they need a rude awakening. Jude's warning is for those who are passive: there is a fight for the faith, so be alert and prepared! To the complicit, he warns: if you continue on this road, it leads to certain death.

We have a responsibility to contend for the faith that has been entrusted to us (v 4). The church today is just as susceptible to power struggles, false and alluring teaching, falling away from the purity of the gospel, and bringing dishonour to the name of Jesus. How aware are we and how prepared are we to contend for the faith?

Lord, have mercy. Christ, have mercy. Help us distinguish true from false; help us discern how best to honour Jesus as Lord and 'be pure and blameless' until Christ returns.[1]

[1] Phil 1:9,10

BIBLE IN A YEAR: Isaiah 37,38; Hebrews 4

Kept by Love and Mercy

'The LORD is my shepherd; I shall not want ... thou art with me; thy rod and thy staff they comfort me.'[1]

Jude is confident that the contrast between truth and apostasy will be clear to the believers. Jesus warned that apostates would come, but that they would be recognisable by their fruit.[2] Jude gives some pointers: apostates are contemptuous about truth and purity (v 18); they're led by their ungodly desires, fanciful dreams (v 8) and natural instincts (v 19); they bring division. They do not have the Spirit of God in them and do not produce the fruit of the Spirit – we must recognise this and have nothing to do with it.

Those who have the Spirit are keen to grow in faith and holiness (v 20) – they produce the fruit of the Spirit. They 'pray in the Spirit' – praying for God's will to be done rather than their own. They keep themselves in God's love, by keeping Jesus' golden rule: love the Lord God by obeying his command and loving each other.[3]

Jude does not want the believers to despair about their church or feel condemned. He knows there are many among them who produce the fruit of the Spirit. He even has a word of hope for those who are falling away: turn back to God, who can keep you in his love and mercy. God's love is the Shepherd's fierce and protective love for his sheep: 'I give them eternal life, and they shall never perish; no one will snatch them out of my hand. My Father, who has given them to me, is greater than all; no one can snatch them out of my Father's hand.'[4] Jude encourages us to show the same fierce love and compassionate mercy to those who are doubting and tempted by false teachers (vs 22,23). Mercy and love can bring people back from the very brink of hell.

Father, keep us in your love and mercy. Help us distinguish what is false. Help us display your love and mercy to doubters and stumblers, drawing them back to you.

---

[1] Ps 23:1,4, KJV [2] Matt 7:15-20 [3] John 15:10-17 [4] John 10:28,29

BIBLE IN A YEAR: **Isaiah 39,40; Psalm 106**

Acts 21:27 – 28:31

TO LIVE IS CHRIST AND TO DIE IS GAIN

The book of Acts starts in Jerusalem, with Jesus' first disciples and the wonderful story of the church's birth. It ends with Paul in Rome, preparing to face Caesar. There is a sense of satisfaction in knowing that the church is growing daily; it is fulfilling its great commission to make disciples of all nations, but it comes with the constant threat of persecution. The challenge at the end of the book, for us, is: 'Will we carry on these great acts of love and service for God and his kingdom, no matter what the cost?'

In Acts 20, the Ephesian Christians weep their farewell to Paul and his companions as he sets his face like flint towards Rome,[1] just as Jesus steeled himself for his last journey to Jerusalem. We will notice echoes of Jesus' journey to Jerusalem and death as we read Paul's interactions with the disciples and the religious and secular leaders. Paul has reconciled himself to death, as Jesus did, and trusts God's plans for him: 'For to me, to live is Christ and to die is gain.'[2] His journey, with his companions, reveals the authenticity of this confession. He rejoiced in serving Jesus his Lord in the mission and shepherding of the church, but he has his eyes on the ultimate prize – eternal fellowship with God.

Paul has gone from zealous persecutor of the Christians to deeply cherished brother and father to many new churches. I love reading how they expressed love for one another – I would love to experience more of that in church life! One of the things that struck me in Acts 21–28, as I prepared these notes, was the new insights into the love, fellowship and family commitment of the early church. Their identity as the people of God, united in the mission of God by the Spirit, the love of the Father and the joy of Christ their Saviour – through suffering as well as success – is a wonderful encouragement and challenge to us today.

Katharine McPhail

---

[1] cf Isaiah 50:7 [2] Phil 1:21

Light in a Dark World

'We also have the prophetic message as something completely reliable ... a light shining in a dark place, until the day dawns and the morning star rises in your hearts.'[1]

Today's passage shows us how controversial Paul was, both for the church in Jerusalem and for the wider Jewish community. Paul and his companions had been kept from entering the province of Asia by the Spirit because God wanted them to preach the gospel in Macedonia.[2] The Jews from Asia had clearly heard about Paul and they knew he was at the heart of the rapid growth of the Way. As the gospel spreads, so does a hostile spirit against it – Jesus warned of this. Luke builds up a sense of foreboding, reminiscent of Jesus' trial and Stephen's martyrdom.

Let's not forget poor Trophimus here. For Gentiles to enter the Temple courts was punishable by death – he was in danger of his life because of this false accusation, even if the accusers were really concerned about stopping Paul.

Today, there are so many examples of hostility to the gospel. There are many, like Trophimus and Paul, caught up in power struggles which endanger their lives. When we preach the gospel and call people to repentance and salvation in Jesus Christ, we will witness people brought from darkness to light, but in doing so we may well encounter fear, misunderstanding and threat. It is especially hard for people like Paul, whose conversion meant alienation from family, culture and religion. The tensions and threats that he experienced can help us to pray for our brothers and sisters in similar situations and for our own testimony in a culture that is often hostile to Christ. Organisations like Open Doors and Barnabas give an insight into how our brothers and sisters around the world are suffering from persecution, even as they rejoice in the gospel.

'Now, Lord, consider their threats and enable your servants to speak your word with great boldness.'[3] Grant us faith, courage and opportunity, Jesus.

[1] 2 Pet 1:19 [2] Acts 16:6–10 [3] Acts 4:29

BIBLE IN A YEAR: **Isaiah 41,42; Hebrews 5**

Psalm 5

Burdened, but Faith-Filled

'I, by your great love, can come into your house' (v 7). Thank you for the sanctuary of your love, Lord, when I am burdened in spirit.

What a wonderful psalm to read on a Sunday before church – even if (or especially because) it is a lament! David sets us an example of a humble heart, burdened but faith-filled. He acknowledges God's sovereignty over his life (v 2); he is expectant that God will listen to him (v 3); he humbly confesses that it is only by God's love that anyone – be he king or shepherd – can enter the presence of the Lord (v 7); he worships the Lord with reverence and a submissive spirit (v 7); he prays for the Lord's righteousness to guide his life (v 8); he trusts in the Lord's righteousness to bring blessing and protection to those who trust in God and obey him (vs 11,12).

It is with this attitude of reverent worship that David brings his prayer of lament. He knows that he needs to share his troubled mind and spirit with the Lord, to ask the Lord for his comfort, wisdom and protection. David is burdened by the world around him, by the sin and wickedness that impact him and God's people. He has seen and experienced so much that is against God's law and righteousness that he cannot bear it. He wants the Lord to act with righteousness against the wickedness he sees around him and is not afraid to ask God to do so.

What have you experienced in your life recently that has grieved you? What do you see and hear in the world around you that burdens your spirit? Let David's psalm inspire your own lament to the Lord. The psalm ends with David's confidence in the love and benevolence of God. Finish your lament with a similar confession of your trust and confidence in God.

I take refuge in you, Lord; I will ever sing for joy. I lay my lament before you and wait expectantly on you.

BIBLE IN A YEAR: **Isaiah 43,44; Hebrews 6**

Jesus Messiah is Lord!

Everything I am and have I offer to you, my only Lord Jesus, my joy and righteousness. What can I say and do to show my love for you today?

Paul is an impressively educated man. He speaks to the Roman officer in Greek and to the crowd in Aramaic, knowing that it is the only way they would listen and understand. He relates to the Roman in a way that will get his attention: Paul is a Roman citizen from an important city. He identifies as Jewish, both to show the Roman that he has the right to speak to the Jewish crowd, but also to calm the crowd and gain their attention. He shows his impressive religious credentials. He understands the passion of the crowd and relates to them. He grounds himself in Jewish tradition and hierarchy, mentioning his relationship to Gamaliel and the Jewish authorities – and he even tells the crowd that he persecuted the church.

The unspoken question is: 'Why would such a zealous Pharisee *turn against* his God and the Law?' The answer is that he did no such thing. Notice how many times he uses the term 'Lord' as he describes his encounter with Jesus on the Damascus road. As a Jew, he worshipped the Lord God: using the term Lord is significant. Jesus Messiah is Lord: Paul recognised this for the first time. He immediately asked the Lord what he should do in response. Paul yearns for his fellow Jews to do the same.

More impressive than Paul's intelligence, however, is his steadfast faith. He is committed to fulfil what the Lord has asked him to do. The Lord had revealed that Paul would preach before Gentile kings and would suffer much for the name of Jesus.[1] Paul had faith that God would complete the work begun in him and did not flinch from sharing in the suffering of Christ. This hostile encounter was one more step on his journey of faith.

What has the Lord called you to do? How are you responding? What testimony do you have to share, about your faith in Jesus? Are you prepared to share it?

[1] Acts 9:15,16

BIBLE IN A YEAR: **Isaiah 45,46; Psalm 107**

Acts 22:12–21

Blinded by the Light

'My luminary, my morning and evening star ... My balance of joy in a world that has gone off joy's standard.'[1]

In verse 11 Paul tells his hearers that he was completely blinded by the light of Jesus. This was literally true, but it speaks into his spiritual state, too. As he must be led physically, so he must seek spiritual guidance from followers of Jesus. Everything he knows about the Lord God has been turned upside down. He cannot rely on his intellect or religious knowledge and zeal. Paul uses both Ananias' testimony and the healing miracle performed by Ananias to persuade the crowd that the God of his ancestors was behind his conversion. God restored Paul's sight, both physically and spiritually. Paul's baptism is another sign of his new obedience, faith and confession of Jesus.

So far the crowd have listened attentively, but the latter part of Paul's speech provokes them violently (v 22). It was not the fact that Paul was baptised in the name of Jesus that stirred them, nor that he was part of a focused attack against Jewish converts like Stephen. They are furious that he claims God judged Jerusalem's lack of faith and sent Paul instead to preach to the Gentiles.

Many converts to Christ have painful testimonies of being rejected by family and community. Accepting Christ and following him can be seen as a rejection of how we are brought up or our community values. Most of us need to work out how we communicate our faith in Jesus among friends, family and colleagues, who may see our faith as a judgement on them. Yet we need to give them an opportunity to hear the gospel. It can scare us to think of people rejecting Jesus and rejecting us, but there is a wonderful possibility that they will see the light of Christ and go from blindness to spiritual sight.

Lord Jesus, fill me with the Spirit of boldness, love and freedom – so I may testify to who you are. Forgive me for my timidity; give me your strength, Lord.

[1] RS Thomas, 'Luminary', in *Uncollected Poems*, Bloodaxe Books, 2013

BIBLE IN A YEAR: Isaiah 47,48; Hebrews 7

Where is Justice?

'Almighty God, by whom kings reign and princes decree justice, and from whom alone cometh all counsel, wisdom and understanding ... send down the heavenly wisdom from above.'[1]

The power dynamics in this passage are fascinating. The Jews use the power of the mob against Paul. The Romans are quite willing to put down mobs with extreme brutal force, but it is clear here that they want to keep the people happy, or at least peaceable. The power of the mob robs Paul of his audience for the gospel, as well as his freedom, and it threatens his physical welfare. That is frightening.

Paul is helpless against the mob's anger, but he has rights as a Roman citizen to secure justice for himself. It is then the Roman commander's turn to be alarmed at the potential consequences of abusing a Roman citizen. It is horrifying how normal it was for the authorities to abuse those who did not have citizen's rights, as is clear from Paul's initial treatment.

Paul's knowledge of justice and citizen's rights is a good example to us. We know only too well from daily news how often power is abused, on a domestic, national and international scale. Some of us will have experienced threats to our freedom and security because of the gospel, but even if we haven't personally, it's true for our brothers and sisters around the world. It is a vital part of our family responsibility to pray against persecution and injustice. We also need to seek justice, to do justice and to speak out for the abused and vulnerable. So many in our society do not have the power that Paul had here when his safety was threatened. How can we be with them and for them so that justice is done? Call to mind an injustice you are aware of: 'Lord, lover of the poor, persecuted and oppressed, I bring (name an area of concern) before your throne. In your mercy, hear my prayer for justice.'

Lord, direct my path to seek justice in my community and steward well what power I have to bring justice for the weak.

[1] William Barclay, 'Prayer of the House of Commons', in *A Barclay Prayer Book*, SCM Press, 2003 (ebook)

BIBLE IN A YEAR: **Isaiah 49,50; Hebrews 8**

Acts 22:30 – 23:11

O Brother, Where art Thou?

"'I was found by those who did not seek me" … concerning Israel he says, "All day long I have held out my hands to a disobedient and obstinate people."'[1]

What was going through Paul's mind as he said 'My brothers' (23:1)? Paul has been one of them, working with the highest authorities on how to persecute the converts to Jesus. He knows people in this room – perhaps he studied and worked with them. We know that Paul longed for his fellow Jews to understand how blind they were about Jesus,[2] but he was also aware of Jesus' warning about how faith in him would turn brother against brother.[3] How careful Jesus had been to urge his disciples to turn the other cheek,[4] to conquer evil with good,[5] to answer with gentleness and respect, knowing how heart-breaking it would be for his beloved disciples to face the hostility of brothers.

Because Paul knows his brothers, he knows their disagreements. When it is clear that his first defence is offensive to them, he drops the resurrection bomb into the room. Perhaps he realises it is the easiest way to show the commander, who has organised this meeting, the contradiction at the heart of the Jewish hostility to Paul: they claim to be righteous but are they displaying the righteousness of God? I wonder what the commander really thinks of it all. Does he pay any attention to the discussion or just their behaviour?

There are bombs we can drop, too: in debates about science and faith, sexuality and identity, genetic research and so on. But *how* (or even if) we drop the bomb and *who* is listening are two really important issues to bear in mind.

May we display your righteousness in the face of trial, opposition and hostility. May we have the discernment, wisdom and gentleness to speak the right word at the right time.

[1] Rom 10:20,21 [2] Rom 10 [3] Matt 10:21 [4] Matt 5:39; Luke 6:29 [5] Rom 12:21 [6] 1 Pet 3:15,16

BIBLE IN A YEAR: **Isaiah 51,52; Hebrews 9**

Favour in a Fragile World

'Lead me, LORD, in your righteousness because of my enemies – make your way straight ... you bless the righteous; you surround them with your favour as with a shield.'[1]

The book of Acts charts the journey of the church's mission from Jerusalem into the heart of the Gentile world: Rome. In 23:11, Christ affirms that Paul is doing the Lord's will, despite the opposition and murderous threat from his Jewish brothers, despite the growing divergence between his culture and the world of the gospel. It is heartbreaking that Paul's testimony includes rejection from the people he most longs to accept the gospel; the city of Jerusalem, which prided itself in being the Lord's dwelling place, rejected God's mission to the world when they rejected Jesus. Paul knows, however, that he is following in his Lord's footsteps and, despite the anguish, he submits to Christ's authority above all others.

The Sanhedrin, who were at war with each other over the resurrection, are united again by a plot to murder Paul. We get an insight into Paul's family here: we already know that he must have come from an influential family because he was a Roman citizen and very well educated; here we see a possible connection between the Sanhedrin and a member of Paul's family. We do not know if Paul's nephew actually had any official loyalty to the Jewish ruling authorities, but in any case, we see that he does not want his uncle murdered: another possible example of conflicting loyalties because of the gospel. The commander, too, shows where his loyalties lie: to Rome and its laws. The commander's integrity is now to Paul's advantage as he commits to protect Paul and do a thorough job. Paul tells us to pray for all in authority over us, even if we don't agree with their politics, religion or morals, so that we can live peaceably.[2] It is good to pray for favour, for those in authority to govern with integrity, and for anything that is harmful to the gospel to be brought to light and thwarted.

Take time to pray for this now, for your nation and local authorities.

[1] Ps 5:8,12 [2] 1 Tim 2:1,2

BIBLE IN A YEAR: **Isaiah 53,54; Psalms 108,109**

Acts 23:23–35

Kingdom Surpasses Empire

'But about the Son he says, "Your throne, O God, will last for ever and ever; a sceptre of justice will be the sceptre of your kingdom."'[1]

The commander is centre stage in this passage and he has the dominating voice until he is replaced by Governor Felix. The commander embroiders the truth somewhat, to protect himself and look like the hero for a day! Luke's narrative describes the seemingly well-oiled and powerful machine that was the Roman Empire. It certainly gives a feel for the power of Rome and what it meant to be a protected citizen of the Roman Empire, as Paul was. We know from church history, however, that Christians often faced terrible persecution from Rome. Until Emperor Constantine, many emperors of Rome were more often brutally against Christianity than they were protective or neutral towards it.

Jesus told Pilate that he and the Roman Empire only had power because God allowed it.[2] He promised his disciples that nothing could prevent him building his church – not the Roman Empire nor the gates of hell.[3] Paul, too, wrote of the sovereignty of God over all other powers.[4] It gave him the faith he needed to face all anxiety and all threats.[5]

Paul's voice is not heard in this passage. He seems powerless against the Roman authorities, but we can be certain that he never stopped praying for himself, his co-workers, the church and his gospel mission, knowing that God is Lord even in the fiercest spiritual warfare and toughest situations. We may feel that the power of this dark world can overcome the gospel and silences our voice, but we trust in the sovereign Lord who hears our prayers and whose plans for the kingdom and the gospel will not be thwarted. All powers and authorities – whether they are sympathetic to the gospel or hostile – will pass away, but Christ's kingdom, power and authority will never pass away.

Pray for the gospel mission in your area and for those who are seeking to share the gospel.

[1] Heb 1:8 [2] John 19:10,11 [3] Matt 16:18 [4] Col 2:9,10 [5] Rom 8:31,39

BIBLE IN A YEAR: **Isaiah 55,56; Hebrews 10**

How Long, O Lord?

Lord, I confess that I am often overwhelmed by the sorrows of the world. So I turn to you, merciful Saviour, trusting that you will hear my prayer.

David has experienced the Lord's anger against him. When he sinned against Bathsheba and Uriah the Hittite, he became aware of the Lord's anger – not only through Nathan's prophetic rebuke[1] but also through his experience of wasting away physically, emotionally and spiritually.[2] It was only when he confessed his sin that the burden of God's anger was removed and he experienced the relief and joy of a contrite heart reconciled to God. We have all experienced this pattern of sin, repentance and reconciliation. God's word encourages us to recognise that the Lord is angry with sin in our life and we submit to his discipline.[3]

David is experiencing God's anger differently here, however. God's anger with the world and with the unrighteous has an impact on those who are trying to walk with him. We can experience this as spiritual groaning against sin and the darkness in the world;[4] we can be directly or indirectly affected by others' sinful behaviour (as David describes here); we can see our loved ones suffer at the hands of others. As with David, it impacts our walk with God, our ability to pray and praise and offer our lives in worship.

What do we do when we are affected by sin and suffering in these ways? David teaches us to turn to God, to lament, to speak out against evil, to intercede in prayer. He also teaches us to confess our faith in God when we feel poor in spirit, to trust in God's steadfast love and to continue to worship.

Lord, may I know your mercy and in turn show your mercy and grace to all – friend and foe – in order to be a child of my heavenly Father.

[1] 2 Sam 12 [2] Ps 32 [3] Heb 12:4–11 [4] Rom 8

BIBLE IN A YEAR: **Isaiah 57,58; Hebrews 11**

Acts 24:1–21

Disturbers of the Peace?

'… we have peace with God through our Lord Jesus Christ, through whom we have gained access by faith into this grace in which we now stand.'[1]

As far as we can tell, Paul was alone to defend himself, with no witnesses – unlike Ananias, who had elders and a lawyer with him (v 1). Paul's life has been threatened and no matter how confident he is that God wants him in Rome, no matter how brilliantly he defends himself, this must be a dreadful, lonely time. Felix is acknowledged both by Ananias (vs 2,3) and Paul (v 10) as having governed his province well and peaceably. Ananias emphasises the threat to peace, accusing Paul of being a disturber of the peace. The false accusation that Paul deliberately desecrated the Temple courts has stuck (v 9). These religious leaders are willing to break one of the Ten Commandments (do not bear false witness against a neighbour) to destroy Paul and the Way. Their justification must have been that they had a higher purpose. The implication in their argument is that 'the Way' (v 14) or the 'Nazarene sect' (v 5) – like other sects

Rome suppressed – is a threat to peace, both for the Jews and for the Roman world.

In many ways this is true – the gospel is a disturber of the world's peace. Jesus did warn us of the disturbing force of the gospel.[2] Throughout history, it has radically changed communities, policies, laws and nations. In the twenty-first century, much of this radical transformation has been reappraised in the light of the horrors of colonialism. It is sad to think that the gospel itself is falsely accused of desecrating human freedom when in fact it is the bringer of peace with God – the hope of humanity – as the trial of Paul exemplifies (v 21).

We are ministers of this gospel. We may face accusations of disturbing people's peace by sharing what we believe, but we have a gospel that brings true peace with God.

Let's follow Paul's example of striving to keep our conscience clear before God and people (v 16).

---

[1] Rom 5:1,2 [2] Matt 10:34,36

BIBLE IN A YEAR: Isaiah 59,60; Psalms 110,111